The Complete Jewish Guide to France

Also by Toni L. Kamins

The Complete Jewish Guide to Britain and Ireland

A
TRAVEL
GUIDE

The Complete
Jewish Guide
to *France*

Toni L. Kamins

St. Martin's Griffin ✖ New York

For Harold, Mom, and Dad

www.stmartins.com

Design by Ralph Fowler

Maps by David Lindroth

Registry of Jews in Marseille, 1808 (pp. 134, 135), reproduced courtesy of the Institut Méditerranéen Mémoire et Archives du Judaïsme, Marseille.

Photograph of the mikvah in Bischheim (p. 181) by Albert Huber; the exterior and interior of the synagogue at Pfaffenhoffen (pp. 184, 185) by F. Luckel; and the Jewish-Alsatian Museum in Bouxwiller (p. 186), reproduced courtesy of the Agence de Développement Touristique du Bas-Rhin. All other photographs are courtesy of the author.

Copy of original title page from an eighteenth-century Chumash published in Metz (p. 203), reproduced courtesy of the Institut Méditerranéen Mémoire et Archives du Judaïsme, Marseille.

Library of Congress Cataloging-in-Publication Data
Kamins, Toni.
    The complete Jewish guide to France/Toni Kamins.
      p. cm.
    ISBN 0-312-24449-5
      1. Jews—France—History.   2. Jews—France—Paris—History.
    3. Judaism—France.   4. Judaism—France—Paris.   5. France—Guide-
    books.   6. Paris (France)—Guidebooks.   7. France—Description and travel.
    8. Paris (France)—Description and travel.   9. Jews—Travel—France–Guide-
    books.   I. Title.
DS135.F83K35 2001
914.404'84—dc21

                                                                    2001031943

First Edition: September 2001

10 9 8 7 6 5 4 3 2 1

Contents

Acknowledgments

My thanks go to Robin Massée and Marion Fourestier of the French Government Tourist Office in New York; Catherine Lehmann of the Agence de Développement Touristique du Bas-Rhin; Corinne Daniel, CRDT Provence; Marie-Yvonne Holley, CRDT Aquitaine; Chantal Marchaland, Office du Tourisme, Aix-en-Provence; Françoise Godebski, Avignon; Sylvie Grange, Musée Judéo-Comtadin, Cavaillon; Danielle Damiani of the Comité Départemental du Tourisme de Vaucluse; Julien Rudloff, Obernai; Pierre Katz, Marmoutier; Béatrice Sommer, Pfaffenhoffen; Annie Trianneau, Colmar; Joan Bloom of Hill and Knowlton; Andy Lazarus, Rail Europe; Sam Gruber, International Survey of Jewish Monuments; Amy Stein-Milford, Eldridge Street Synagogue; Tom Shachtman; Ralph Goldman and Freda Weiss, American Joint Distribution Committee; Karen Fawcett, Bonjour Paris; Shelley List, jewishtravel.com; Laurent David Cohen; Sukey Pett; and Maribeth Clemente.

Many people in the Jewish community in France, along with several individuals who work for its many organizations, received me with enthusiasm and were extremely generous with their time and knowledge. My thanks go to Annie Rayskie Rappoport, Fondation du Judaïsme Français; Arielle Weintraub, Musée d'Art et d'Histoire du Judaïsme, Paris; Claude-Sabin Nadjari, Institut Méditerranéen Mémoire et Archives du Judaïsme, Marseille; Jean-Paul Marx, Sélestat; Robert Milhaud, Aix-en-Provence; Rabbi Moché Amar, Avignon; Rabbi Jacky Amar, Carpentras; Jean-

Claude Neymann, Entreprises René Neymann, Wasselonne; Madame Claude Bloch, Commission Patrimoine B'nai B'rith, Strasbourg; Rabbi Jacky Dreyfuss, Chief Rabbi of the Upper Rhine and the Consistoire Israélite du Haut-Rhin.

Rabbi Seth Frisch and Rabbi Eugene Markovitz read pieces of the manuscript and gave me many generous and insightful comments; Rabbi Leon Wengrovsky took the time to answer questions on Jewish law with great patience.

I am grateful to New York's Writers Room, where this book was really born, for providing me with a very hard-to-come-by commodity in New York: a quiet place to work, free from distraction; and to the Brydcliffe Colony for the Arts in Woodstock, New York, which gave me a residency during the crucial first few months of this project.

My thanks to Andrew Miller and Greg Cohn, former editors at St. Martin's Press, who first gave the green light to the project; to my editors, Kristen Macnamara and Joanna Jacobs, who saw the project through to completion, patiently I might add; and to my agent, Carolyn Krupp of IMG Literary, who has at least as much patience.

Thanks to the monthly dinner group: Dan Hurley, Norman Schreiber, Erica Manfred, Minda Zetlin, Marion Betancourt, Florence Isaacs, Linda Konner, Joan Iaconnetti, and Janet Bailey.

Special thanks go to Charles Ruas, whose encouragement was ever present on two continents, and to Adrian Leeds for her limitless supply of ideas.

As always, my family was around to provide support while they eagerly awaited publication: My parents, Walter and Judith Kamins; and my sisters, brothers-in-law, nieces, and nephews Erica, Nick, and Conor Farrell; Jennifer, Richard, Marissa, Tamara, and Jake Bullock; and Dana and Jeff Jacobs.

Even as a writer I am at a loss to find the words that express adequately my appreciation to my husband, Harold Itzkowitz. Without his love, support, and valuable criticism, this, along with many other things, would not have been possible.

Introduction

Like most Americans, American Jews come from someplace else. It may have been our parents, grandparents, great-grandparents, or even further back than that, but at some point our families lived in some other country. The vast majority of our families come from one or more European countries, and it is for that reason that this series of Complete Jewish Guides begins with the countries that make up both western and eastern Europe.

To many American Jews, European Jewish history begins and ends with the Holocaust—the Shoah, that series of events that took place between 1939 and 1945 during World War II. But there is so much more to European Jewish history than that. As you will discover in each country covered in this series, Jews have lived in Europe for some two thousand years—way before Adolf Hitler and his Nazis. And they continue to live and thrive there today despite them.

Visiting Jewish communities around the world is an age-old Jewish tradition. Throughout the centuries travelers and emissaries have chronicled the Jewish communities of their day and visited the synagogues, cemeteries, and other landmarks of their coreligionists. Though there was in centuries past a very strong religious component to the work of those emissaries, the interest in the legacy of Jews in various parts of the world is not exclusively religious in nature. It is also a means of forming a cultural connection between Jews from one part of the world and Jews in another. And it can be a bridge between past, present, and future.

From the fall of Jerusalem in A.D. 70 until the founding of Israel in 1948, the Jewish people were without an official country. Persecution, murder, high taxes, ghettos were all a part of life for Jews in Europe. But wherever they lived during the great Diaspora, they left their traditions in the form of synagogues, schools, monuments, neighborhoods, and cultural institutions. It is through those that today's traveler, veteran or first timer, can become better acquainted with the vibrant Jewish communities that rose from the ashes and learn about their neighborhoods, institutions, and centuries-old culture.

So come along with me on a journey of rediscovery. I promise you won't be disappointed.

—TONI L. KAMINS
New York City
September 2001

Travel Basics

Getting to France

ALONG WITH AIR FRANCE, many U.S. airlines have daily direct flights to Paris. Air France and Delta also fly nonstop from New York to Nice and Lyon. You can take connecting flights to other French cities from those destinations.

Air France: 800-237-2747

Delta: 800-323-2323

American: 800-433-7300

Continental: 800-231-0856

Getting Around France

TRAINS

Intercity travel in France is best accomplished by train. Trains are fast, frequent, comfortable, and relatively inexpensive even in first class. The high-speed TGVs (trains à grande vitesse) reach most areas of the country, especially if you're using Paris as a hub. No major city is more than four and a half hours from the capital.

There are two ways to buy train tickets before you leave home.

1. Rail Europe is the U.S. representative for all the European railroads and can sell you tickets for anywhere you want to go on the continent, including the Eurostar between London and Paris.
    Tel: 888-382-7245, hours: M–F 9 A.M.–9 P.M. www.raileurope.com/us. In addition to selling Eurailpasses, Europasses, single tickets, and other travel services, they have various passes just for France.

2. You can reserve tickets and seats (including for the Eurostar) directly from the French National Railroad Web site provided you can pick tickets up in France (at any train station) or another European country within a few days of making your reservation. You pay for them when you pick them up and major credit cards are accepted. Alternatively, you can pay for them online with a credit card and have them mailed to your hotel or other address in France; admittedly this carries a small risk. Purchasing tickets through the Web site, whether you pick them up or have them mailed to your hotel, might have some price benefit because you can take advantage of various excursion fares, senior citizen fares, and so on that are not available in the United States. See www.sncf.fr, click on the British flag for an English version.

Note: Buying a ticket on a particular train guarantees you passage. It does not guarantee you a seat. The seat reservation is a few francs extra. If you buy a ticket for passage without a seat reservation you'll have to look for a seat on the train that does not have a reservation ticket on it. That indicates that it hasn't been reserved.

CARS

A car might prove useful for a full tour of the Jewish sights in the provinces (especially Alsace, Provence, and Bordeaux), and it might be lots of fun as well. French roads are well marked and maps like Michelin's and Blay-Foldex's add to the relative ease of getting around. I have three pieces of advice regarding car rental in France: (1) Reserve and pay before you leave home; it's cheaper. (2) Make sure you reserve a car with an automatic shift. Standard shift cars are still the norm in Europe and if you're not accustomed to driving one, you shouldn't make your vacation the time to get reacquainted with the clutch and the shift. (3) Rent from a reputable firm; some suggestions are listed below. Remember that gas (essence) is more expensive in France than it is at home, even in the high-priced summer of 2001, and it is measured in liters.

Auto Europe: 888-223-5555; www.autoeurope.com/

Hertz: 800-654-3001; www.hertz.com/

Avis: 800-230-4898

Getting Around Paris

DON'T EVEN THINK ABOUT renting a car here. Parking is impossible and if you don't know the city, well . . . trust me, you don't need a car. If you're starting your trip in Paris and want to rent a car to get to another part of the country, rent it just before you go.

Even if you're only spending a short time in Paris you will want to get a copy of a small book known generically as *Paris par Arrondissement*. It lists every street, its closest Métro stop, and the streets where it begins and ends. There is also a map of each arrondissement (an administrative district of which Paris is divided into twenty), a Métro map, a bus map, listings of bus routes, embassies, monuments, museums, and so on. It's just indispensable; even the Parisians carry it around. In fact, many editions are called just that—*L'Indispensable*. It's available at many newspaper/magazine kiosks, most bookstores, and newspaper and magazine shops.

MÉTRO PASS

If you're going to be in Paris for more than a few days you'll want to buy a pass that allows you unlimited access on the Métro and the bus. Prices vary according to duration and some passes require a passport-sized photo. The Paris Métro and bus system is the best way to get around town and it's easy to use. You can buy these passes at any Métro stop with cash or credit card.

MUSEUM PASS

You can spend months going to museums in Paris—museums of every type. If this is your plan you'll want to get the Carte Musées et Monuments. It has varying durations and is priced accordingly, but it allows you unlimited museum access for that time period and it frequently allows you in at the head of the line. Purchase these at museums and also at Métro stations. Many museums will allow you to pay in advance for a visit on Shabbat—the Louvre among them. Ask at the museum's information desk.

Telephones

*F*RENCH TELEPHONE AND FAX numbers all have ten digits and each region has its own prefix (included in the ten digits) beginning with 0. Cell phone numbers begin with 06; toll-free numbers (known as green numbers) begin with 08. Paris phone numbers begin with 01. To call within France dial the entire ten-digit number including the 0 even when you're in the region you are calling.

To call from outside France dial 011 (the international access code), 33 (the country code for France), and then the phone number minus the zero. So, for example, to call Paris from the United States dial 011-33-1-12-34-56-78; to call Strasbourg dial 011-33-3-12-34-56-78, and so on.

PUBLIC PHONES

Pay phones are all over the place and they're easy to use. There are essentially four ways to use them, all of which involve some type of card.

1. Prepaid phone cards (télécarte) from the post office or Métro station are available in 50-unit and 120-unit denominations and are embedded with a computer chip. Pick up the receiver, slide the card into the slot near the bottom of the phone with the chip facing up, wait for the digital display to show you how many units the card has left, and then wait for it to prompt you to dial. Once you're connected the units will count down.

2. Other prepaid phone cards that use a toll-free access number are available from tabacs—cafés that sell tobacco—and from some newsstands. With these cards

you dial a toll-free number—called a nombre vert, or green number—and then follow the voice prompts. But please note that the voice prompts will be in French.

3. Pay phones take major credit cards. Follow the instructions on the information card on the phone— they're in several languages.

4. Use your personal telephone credit card by following your service provider's instructions.

Money

*U*NTIL JANUARY 2002, WHEN the Euro starts to circulate, the coin of the republic is still the French franc. Notes are in 10-, 20-, 50-, 100-, and 500-franc denominations; coins are 1, 2, 5, 10, and 20 francs, 1, 5, 10, and 20 centimes, and one-half franc (50 centimes). You will, however, see prices for everything in both Euros and francs, and if you pay by credit card you may see the charges converted from Euros on your statement. Save your receipts and compare them to the amounts on your statement.

Cash machines are omnipresent in all but the smallest towns and traveler's checks are really a thing of the past when you're coming to France. Use the ATMs just as you do at home. Just be sure that your personal identification number (PIN) is four digits (if your PIN is longer have your bank change it), and if you only know your PIN in letters memorize it in its numerical form because French ATM keypads are numbers only. One thing more to note: At ATMs at home you have a choice of withdrawing cash from either your checking or saving accounts, but outside the country you won't have that choice. The funds will be withdrawn from whichever account is the primary account, which is usually checking. So make sure there is enough money in that account to cover your withdrawals.

Hotels

Note: All of the hotels listed in this section are well maintained; have private bath, minibar, telephone, television (with cable and CNN), in-room safe-deposit box, hair dryer, and elevator; are open all year (unless otherwise noted); and accept all major credit cards. Hotels in the expensive category also have room service, concierge, laundry service, and the other amenities one expects in a hotel of that class. Hotels listed as expensive are $250 per room per night and over, but specials may bring the price down a bit; moderate hotels are $150 and up. Hotels outside of Paris will be a bit lower and exact prices will vary with currency fluctuations. These are all personal recommendations.

PARIS

Expensive

Hôtel Pavillon de la Reine. 28, place des Vosges. Tel: 01-40-29-19-19. Fax: 01-40-29-19-20.

> You can't beat the location on the lovely place des Vosges and right in one of the main Jewish quarters. The décor in this excellent hotel is oh so romantic.

Villa Beaumarchais. 5, rue des Arquebusiers. Tel: 01-40-29-14-00. Fax: 01-40-29-19-01.

Within walking distance of one of the main Jewish quarters, this charming hotel has very small but well-appointed and well-designed rooms in a central and trendy location. Excellent service.

Hôtel Lutétia. 45, boulevard Raspail. Tel: 01-49-54-46-46.
Fax: 01-49-54-46-00.

One of the few large first-class hotels on the Left Bank, Lutétia enjoys an excellent location down the block from the Bon Marché department store and near St.-Germain-des-Prés. It has the distinction of having served as Gestapo headquarters during the occupation. People tend to have strong opinions about this large Art Deco hotel: They either love it or hate it, and its past is not part of the equation. Some of the rooms on the lower end of the price scale can be a bit spare and frowzy, but in the mid and upper ranges they can be quite lovely. All are larger than your average Paris hotel rooms. Ask to see the room before you accept it and don't be afraid to protest if you don't like what you see— especially in off-season.

Hôtel Millennium Opéra. 12, boulevard Haussmann.
Tel: 01-49-49-16-00. Fax: 01-49-49-17-00.
www.stay.with-us.com.

This first-class hotel in the heart of commercial Paris recently underwent a multimillion-dollar renovation, and it shows in every detail. The rooms in this elegant and comfortable hotel are nicely furnished, though the standard rooms are small, which is not unusual in Paris even in a hotel of this class. Bathrooms are very well appointed. Nearby are the Jewish quarter of the 9th arrondissement, major department stores, and lots of other shopping. Located on one of the grands boulevards and near the Opéra Garnier, the hotel is convenient to everything. And though many rooms face the noisy boulevard Haussmann, you won't hear a thing; I've rarely seen such great window soundproofing. This is a good place to stay if you're coming or going on the Eurostar: It's just minutes from the Gare du Nord.

Moderate

Hôtel Bretonnerie. 22, rue Ste-Croix-de-la-Bretonnerie.
Tel: 01-48-87-77-63. Fax: 01-42-77-26-78. Closed
from July 1 to August 28.

Clean, well-kept, family-run hotel with decent-sized rooms in a city known for its small hotel rooms.

Hôtel Caron de Beaumarchais. 12, rue Vieille-du-Temple.
Tel: 01-42-72-34-12. Fax: 01-42-72-34-63.

A jewel of a hotel in a great neighborhood. Family run and very popular so book way in advance.

Résidence Henri IV. 50, rue des Bernardins.
Tel: 01-44-41-31-81. Fax: 01-46-33-93-22.

In a great location just off the very central rue des Écoles, this clean, small Latin Quarter hotel has typically small rooms, but they all have kitchenettes. If you want more space, ask for an apartment—a bedroom with a separate sitting room, which can accommodate another person if need be. The place Maubert outdoor food market is just three blocks away.

STRASBOURG

Moderate

Hôtel Beaucour. 5, rue Bouchers. Tel: 03-88-76-72-00.
Fax: 03-88-76-72-60.

Charming and centrally located small hotel decorated in traditional Alsatian style. The suites are particularly lovely and spacious.

AVIGNON

Expensive

Hôtel Mirande. 4, place Amirande.
Tel: 04-90-85-93-93. Fax: 04-90-86-26-85.

Centrally located near the Palais des Papes in an old cardinal's residence, this first-rate hotel is comfortable and has wonderful service.

Moderate

Mercure Cité des Papes. 1, rue J. Vilar.
Tel: 04-90-86-22-45. Fax: 04-90-27-39-21.

Centrally located near the Palais des Papes, this typical branch in the Mercure chain has comfortable rooms and good service.

BORDEAUX

Moderate–Expensive

Hôtel Burdigala. 115, rue G. Bonnac.
Tel: 05-56-90-16-16. Fax: 05-56-93-15-06.

Charming hotel with nice rooms and good service and in the center of town.

How to Use This Book

The Book's Structure

THE FIRST CHAPTER OF *The Complete Jewish Guide to France* is designed to give you a historical overview of the history of the Jewish people in France even before you get to the travel part. I've done this so that you will better understand the context of the sights you will be seeing. Each regional chapter contains a shorter but more detailed history of the Jewish communities. Having already read the introductory chapter you will then be able to put the regional information into a broader context and emerge with as full a picture as possible (within the limits of a historical travel guide) of the historical and social fabric surrounding the buildings, museums, synagogues, cemeteries, neighborhoods, and even churches you visit. It is within those sections that you will find individual cities and towns and their Jewish sights.

The Resource Sections

AT THE END OF EACH regional chapter, and each arrondissement section in Paris, you will find lists of resources. These are meant mainly for observant Jewish travelers who require kosher food, places to pray, and other necessities like mikvaot (ritual baths), but they also contain lists of Jewish bookstores and other establishments that the nonobservant and non-Jewish traveler should feel free to visit. Even if you don't keep kosher, a good Jewish meal might be just what you're looking for—a little chicken soup for the soul, as it were. Some towns and cities have no kosher food available at all, and in some places it may be only available at the synagogue or Jewish community center. In those situations a call to the synagogue might result in an invitation to someone's home for a meal, especially on Shabbat.

I have also provided a section on keeping kosher in France, which contains specific information on the various authorities that supervise kosher food, instructions on how to ascertain that the bread you want to buy is kosher, and information about how to buy packaged food that is kosher but may not have any identifying marks on the label. For those of you who eat fish in nonkosher restaurants, I have also included a list of kosher fish.

Cemeteries

THERE ARE DOZENS OF old Jewish cemeteries in France—some going back to the fifteenth century. Some are still in use and others have not been used in many years. In most cases the cemeteries are locked and gated to prevent vandalism.

In small towns or rural areas the Jewish cemeteries are not easy to get to. They are often located on hilly and rocky land—that was not fit for other uses—in very out-of-the-way places. Frequently they have no specific address and you'll need an appointment with the caretaker or somebody from the local Jewish community for a visit. In every instance I have listed a contact number for the cemetery or the name or phone number of someone either within the

Jewish community or at the local tourist office who can help you. This is not a formal process, but it's best to call a few days ahead to see if you can reach someone. When the number listed is for a local tourist office you'll find people who are accustomed to dealing with inquiries and who probably speak some English. When the call is to the local synagogue or cemetery caretaker you may not reach anyone on the first phone call—but try again. Answering machines are not as common in France as they are in the United States, and you may not always find someone who speaks English; Hebrew may help when dealing with a member of the local Jewish community. In larger cities, and also where the cemetery is open, the caretaker will probably stop you and ask why you are there. Don't take offense; it's his job to make sure that visitors are there for a legitimate purpose and to guard against vandalism, which is a problem in Jewish cemeteries in France. If you want to take photos, ask permission first— but, because it is a matter of privacy for the families of the dead, permission is not always granted. Many of the oldest headstones are severely weather-beaten and difficult if not impossible to read; most inscriptions on older stones are in Hebrew.

PARISIAN CEMETERIES

During the nineteenth century, once civil rights for Jews were achieved, Parisian Jews began to bury their dead in the same cemeteries as non-Jews. So the graves of many famous Jews are located in the same places as those of other famous Frenchmen. Information on Parisian cemeteries is located in the individual Paris chapters.

The Mikvah

THE MIKVAH (MIKVÉ IN French, plural is mikvaot), or ritual bath, is a crucial part of any Jewish community—more so even than a synagogue because Jews can pray anywhere ten worshipers are present. The word literally means "a gathering of water." Immersion in the mikvah is usually misunderstood by non-Jews and many nonobservant Jews because it is thought of solely as a ritual through which a woman becomes physically clean after her monthly period so that she may again have sex with her husband—but there's more to it. This ritual immersion, known as tevila, is spiritual rather than physical, and it goes back to biblical times. The process is necessary to achieve a state of tahara (spiritual purification) and without it one remains in a state of tuma (spiritual impurity). In fact, a woman must have already showered or bathed completely before she goes to the mikvah—including removing dirt from under her nails. Men use the mikvah too. It is common in many Hasidic communities for men to go to the mikvah before the Sabbath and before Rosh Hashanah and Yom Kippur; again, the key is a spiritual purification. Immersion in a mikvah is necessary to complete the process of conversion to Judaism. There is also another mikvah known as a kelim mikvah, which purifies glass and metal dishes and utensils purchased from a non-Jew.

There are numerous regulations and laws that apply to the construction of the mikvah; they're derived from a passage in Vayikra (Leviticus). Whether or not you approve of the practice, or agree with the explanation of its purpose, an appreciation of it, as well as the way observant Jews differentiate between physical and spiritual purity, is necessary to an understanding of why the mikvah is one of the most important resources for a community, and why you will see so many old ones throughout France.

Useful French Words and Phrases

kosher—casher

cemetery—le cimetière

meat—la viande

dairy—les produits laitiers

I'm looking for—je cherche

    a kosher restaurant—un restaurant casher

    the Jewish cemetery—le cimetière juif

    the caretaker—le gardien

    the synagogue—la synagogue

    the rabbi—Monsieur le Rabbin

    the Jewish community center—le centre communautaire juif

    the Jewish bookstore—la librairie juive

Keeping Kosher

If you keep kosher you won't go hungry in France. In Paris, for example, there are probably more kosher eateries than even in New York City. Oh they're not all fancy shmancy restaurants with fine table linen (most are of the pizza-and-falafel type), but there is enough variety in both cuisine and price to keep you busy for your entire vacation and then some. In other regions of France you will have to do a little planning, but with large observant communities in areas like Provence and Alsace you'll be well served.

For the most part kosher food is under the supervision of the Beth Din of the local *consistoire*. (The Consistoire Central de France is the central Jewish religious authority in France.) In some cases Lubavitch or a local rabbi also supervises food. Jews who observe kashrus can feel comfortable about buying or eating in places supervised by the local Beth Din. Each Beth Din is run by the regional *consistoire* and is strictly Orthodox. Kosher food stores and restaurants are required to display their certificate prominently in their window or near the front of the shop. There are, in addition, some other organizations and rabbis that have their own hashgacha. The Consistoire publishes a magazine called *Le Cachère* that lists various foodstuffs and kosher establishments. It's available from the *consistoire* (01-40-82-26-13) and from many kosher grocery stores.

The restaurants and takeout places listed in this guide are all under the supervision of the Beth Din. In Paris, listed eateries are under Beth Din supervision and/or the supervision of Rabbi M. Rottenberg, the chief rabbi of Paris's Orthodox rabbinate.

For this cornucopia of kashrus we can thank our Sephardic brethren and the decline of French colonialism in North Africa. It was in the wake of that political debacle that North African Jews began settling in Paris (and other parts of France) in great numbers. The Sephardim from North Africa are also responsible for the renaissance of Jewish communities in towns and cities in southern France that had lost their last Jews decades before.

If you venture into a supermarché (supermarket) in Paris or any other place (and you should just for the cultural experience) you will be hard-pressed to find packaged food with the familiar kosher symbols, or even any kosher symbols. But that's because many products that are kosher don't require special labeling in France. The Paris Beth Din (01-40-82-26-26) will give you a list of nonlabeled foodstuffs that are in fact kosher. Outside of Paris, a local synagogue can give you the same information. Supermarkets also sell fresh fruit and fresh vegetables, which, as any veteran kosher traveler knows, can serve as the mainstay in a kosherly challenged town. And don't forget the open-air street markets for fruit and vegetables.

As far as bread is concerned, the French government monitors the production of this wonderful stuff and if you ask for a baguette (those long crusty loaves of quintessential French bread) fabriquée non moulée (not made in the same pan as anything else) in any boulangerie (bakery) it will be okay to eat. But you must be certain that you buy it from a bakery where the bread is made on the premises and not from a shop or supermarket that sells commercially baked baguettes. So look for une boulangerie artisanale, à l'ancienne, or one that says FABRICATION MAISON. These are bakeries where the bread is handmade on the premises. Boulangeries that say they are artisanale must be so according to French law. These rules apply only to baguettes. Croissants, brioches, and any other kinds of bread should be purchased from a kosher bakery to be on the safe side. Though butter is a main ingredient in many breads, particularly croissants, lard or other shortening is often used too.

Wine is sold in wine shops, supermarkets, and small grocery stores. Kosher wine is readily available in Jewish neighborhoods (and even in places like la Grande Epicerie in the Bon Marché department store; see the 7th Arrondissement section of chapter 2) and will have the same Hebrew markings with which you are already familiar. In a good wine shop or supermarket in a Jewish neighborhood you will find, along with Israeli wines, some very good kosher French wines that you probably won't see at home because they aren't exported.

The ice cream in the Häagen-Dazs shops is kosher, and shops can be found throughout Paris and the rest of the country. Stick to plain ice cream because the toppings, including whipped cream (crème chantilly), are frequently not kosher. Ben and Jerry's ice cream is also kosher and there are a number of Ben and Jerry's shops in Paris. Again, stick to the plain ice cream.

If you're confused about the small-food-shop nomenclature, here's a guide. A boulangerie is a bakery that sells some pastry; a pâtisserie is a pastry shop that sells some bread and candy; a confiserie is a candy shop that sells some pastry; an épicerie is a small grocery store; a supermarché is a supermarket; a boucherie is a butcher shop that sells meat, some poultry (volaille), and some prepared foods and groceries; a fromagerie is a cheese shop that sells some other dairy products, including eggs; a laiterie is a diary shop that sells milk, butter, eggs, and some cheese; and a charcuterie is a shop that sells prepared foods and a few groceries. Don't forget France's open-air markets, where you can pick up fruit, vegetables, and sometimes hard-boiled eggs (oeufs durs).

And finally, you can purchase Shabbat candles in any Jewish neighborhood. If they aren't readily visible just ask for "des bougies pour Chabbat." But note that Paris does not have an eruv.

In addition to the places listed in this guide, here are some Web sites that list Parisian and provincial kosher restaurants along with their addresses, phone numbers, type of food, and hash-gacha.

www.geocities.com/NapaValley/2621

Kosher restaurants in Paris and throughout France. An
   Orthodox Jew and Parisian named David Laurent Cohen
   runs this and he regularly updates it.

www.col.fr/paris_rest.html

List of Parisian restaurants under Beth Din supervision.

www.col.fr/paris/paris_restpro.html

List of provincial restaurants under Beth Din supervision.

The Consistoire de Paris has its own Web site at
   www.consistoire.org with information on its activities and
   links to sites with kosher restaurants and other Jewish
   organizations. There is an English version, but as of the
   time of publication of this book it was not as complete as
   the French.

Kosher Fish

*F*OR THOSE WHO WILL eat fish in nonkosher restaurants, here is a list of French terms for kosher fish that you
may find on a menu.

l'aiglefin (also églefin)—haddock

l'albacore (see thon)—tuna

l'alose—shad

les anchois—anchovies

le bar—sea bass

le barbeau or barbot—barbel

la barbue—brill

la bonite—bonito

la brême—bream

le brochet—pike

le cabillaud—cod

la carpe—carp, but not to be confused with carpe à cuir, which is not kosher. Also, with any carp, verify the presence of scales, as carp in some stages don't have them.

le colin—whiting

la daurade—sea bream, gray, red, or royale

les éperlans—smelts

le flétan—halibut

le goujon—a small lake fish

le grenadier

le grondin

le hareng—herring

la julienne—similar to whiting

le lieu—pollack

la limande-sole—lemon sole

la limande-plie—lemon plaice (similar to sole)

la lotte—monkfish

le loup—sea bass, but not loup de mer, which is not kosher

le maquereau—mackerel

le merlan—another kind of whiting

le merlu or merluche—hake

la morue—cod

la mostelle—a small Mediterranean fish

le mulet—mullet

l'ombrine—char (similar to salmon)

l'orphie—garfish

le pageot

le pagre

le patudo

la perche—perch

la plie—plaice

le prêtre

la rascasse—scorpion fish

le rouget barbet—red mullet

le sandre—pike perch

le sar doré or sargue

les sardines—sardines

le saumon—salmon, but not the same as saumonette, which
 is dogfish, popular on French menus, and not kosher

la sole

le sprat—like herring

le tacaud

la tanche—tench

le thon—tuna

la truite—trout

la truite saumonée—salmon trout

le véron

la vieille

la vivanneau

la vive or le dragon de mer

CHAPTER ONE

A Short History of Jewish France

Early and Medieval France

I F   W E   T H I N K   A B O U T   European Jewish history at all, most of us don't associate France with a significant part of that history. However, there have been Jews in France since the earliest years of the Common Era, and in terms of Jewish scholarship, France was one of the most important centers of European Jewish life—the home of world-famous rabbis and yeshivas, including Rabbi Shlomo Itzchaki (Solomon, son of Isaac), known by the acronym Rashi. To this day, Rashi is considered one of the greatest commentators on the Torah.

The sweep of Jewish history in France begins nearly two millennia ago. Though very early evidence of Jewish settlement in

France is sketchy at best, and abundant hard physical evidence doesn't really crop up until the fifth century, there is enough to point to the existence of a Jewish community or at least groups of Jews in France in those earliest times. There are even some documents that indicate that Jews may have lived in such geographically disparate cities as Metz, Poitiers, and Avignon as early as the first and fourth centuries. From the fifth century, historians have recognizable evidence of Jewish settlement in Brittany, Clermont-Ferrand, Narbonne, Agde, Valence, and Orléans.

From the fifth century until 751, the Merovingians, a dynasty of Frankish kings, ruled part of France. Clovis I (481–511), founder of the monarchy and grandson of the Franks' chief, Meroveus, converted to Catholicism in 496 and with him most of the rest of the population. Of course this meant that Jews living in the kingdom at the time would have come under the same pressure to convert, and the alternatives to conversion were far from attractive. Bishop Avitus of Clermont-Ferrand, for example, offered the five hundred Jews of his town a choice between baptism and expulsion. That tactic was repeated throughout the Franks' kingdom. Most Jews chose expulsion. Some evidence suggests that a later Merovingian king, Dagobert I (612–39), tried the convert-or-get-out strategy, too, but no details are known about this.

Despite the difficulties—only a taste of what was to come over the next centuries—there was a significant increase in the Jewish population of France in this early period, arising from immigration of Jews from Italy, Spain, and other parts of the Roman Empire, and conversions to Judaism among slaves and members of the poorer classes.

The seventh century saw the demise of the Merovingians and the rise of the Carolingian dynasty under Pépin le Bref (Pépin the Short). Though the dynasty would die out in France by 987, this period proved to be a good one for the kingdom's Jews. It was Pépin's son Charlemagne (Charles the Great) who, through his invasion of Italy to support Pope Leo III, his Christianizing of the Saxons, and his conquest of northern Spain and Bavaria, laid the groundwork for the Holy Roman Empire. As emperor, Charlemagne reigned over a kingdom in which intellectual and artistic pursuits flourished, and with them, the kingdom's Jews. So complete was Jewish integration into the economy that they did business with the royal court, held imperial ambassadorships, and worked in the administration of Catholic organizations. Jews even produced wine for the Mass—viticulture being an almost exclusively Jewish occupation at the time.

During that period, there was a real disparity among attitudes of the king, the locals, and Church officials concerning the Jews. Try as it might, the organized Church was largely unsuccessful in its efforts to stir up anti-Jewish sentiment among the populace, and historians point to this lack of success as evidence of friendly personal and professional relations between Jews and Christians. For example, the Church councils of Meux and Paris in 845 and 846 C.E. tried to implement anti-Jewish legislation, but King Charles the Bald (840–77) would have none of it. Later, on both ends of the eleventh century, Bishops Fulbert and Ivo gave anti-Jewish sermons, promulgated anti-Jewish canons, and preached against Jewish influence in the town of Chartres, near Paris. Neither bishop was taken very seriously.

But that would not always be the case.

For many centuries French Jewry was at the forefront of Jewish scholarship, and in the eleventh century it began to come into its own. The centers of French Jewish learning were in both northern (Troyes) and southern (Narbonne) France. Jewish scholars produced commentaries on the Talmud and on the Torah, and discussions of rabbinical decisions and Jewish liturgy. Those works were the talk of the Jewish scholarly world, and in some cases the Christian, too.

Rashi

Ra(Rabbi)Sh(lomo)I(tzchaki) (1040–1105), the son of a scholarly Jewish family, was born in Troyes, once the capital of

Champagne. After going to school in Troyes and then the Talmudic academies of Mainz and Worms (Germany), where he studied with the great Jewish scholars of the time, he returned home and eventually founded his own school. His teachings on the Torah and the Talmud became so renowned that he attracted a considerable following among contemporary Jewish scholars.

Rashi wrote down extensive and laboriously detailed explanations and analyses (known as commentaries) of the texts of the Torah and the Talmud, including a grammar by which they could be studied. Up until this point much scholarly and rabbinical discourse and interpretation was not generally written down, so Rashi's work was groundbreaking, and considering the complexity and enormous length of both the Torah and the Talmud, his work was nothing short of amazing.

The Tosafists

Rashi's students, sons, and sons-in-law continued with his work by commenting on his commentaries. The Hebrew word tosafot means "additions." Rashi's followers used Rashi's own work as a point of departure for additional analysis so that it would become the standard for the study of the Torah and the Talmud within their own schools of rabbinical study.

What made the work of the Tosafists so revolutionary was that through it, Jewish scholars had, for the first time, a logical method of studying Rashi, and through a process of questioning, analyzing, and comparing his writings, they gained greater access to the Torah and the Talmud. As a result they were able to make new and additional interpretations of Jewish law, refine or rethink conclusions to problems arising from its legal texts, and they could themselves provide the impetus for further work in generations to come.

As has been often the case in Jewish history, great scholarship was produced in the midst of turmoil within the Jewish community. In this instance it resulted from riots and other violence whipped up against the Jews prior to the Crusades. The catalyst was an accusation that the Jews of Orléans had conspired with the ruler of Jerusalem, Sultan al-Hakim, to destroy the Church of the Holy Sepulcher. The riots were incited by the clergy and supported by Robert the Pious (King Robert II, 996–1031), who aroused public frenzy. The resulting murders, expulsions, and forced baptisms of Jews ceased only when Pope John XVIII (1004–9) intervened at the behest of Jacob ben Jekuthiel, a prominent Jew of the time.

During the early years of the First Crusade (1096–99), the daily life of Jews in Europe was not adversely affected. And when anti-Jewish events did occur it was the Jews of Germany who bore the brunt. But the very first of these events, murder and forced conversion, took place in France in the cities of Metz and Rouen.

In Rouen, the Crusades served as a pretext for the persecutors. To paraphrase a contemporary sentiment, Why go all the way to the Orient (as the Middle East was known) to kill the defilers of our holy sites when we have those same people right here among us? So in 1144 Louis VII expelled all Jews who had converted to Christianity and then returned to Judaism. It was to be the first of many such expulsions.

In the days before modern communication, one of the ways Jewish communities knew about other Jewish communities was through travelers' tales and messengers from one community to another. One such traveler, Benjamin of Tudela (in Spain), chronicled the known Jewish world in the late twelfth century. His journals provide valuable insight about the lives of contemporary Jews and their communities. His figures, for example, tell us that there were more than six thousand Jews in Narbonne, and that Jews inhabited some 150 towns in the Ile de France (the area around Paris).

Like other countries, France was no stranger to one of the most despicable ongoing lies concocted against Jews over the centuries: the blood libel, also known as ritual murder.

The Blood Libel

*Employed throughout history as a pretext for the murder and
persecution of Jews, the blood libel alleges that Jews hunt and
kill Christians (usually children) and use their blood in the bak-
ing of Passover matzo and for other religious rituals. It has its
origins in the notion that Jews hate people in general and Christians and Christianity in particular. In addition, it takes some
of its power from the superstition that Jews are not human and
have to resort to potions so that they may appear human.*

*The myth of the ritualistic use of human blood by Jews goes
back to ancient times when pagans, who used blood in sacrifices
(a practice forbidden to Jews), misunderstood the Jewish ritual
of removing all blood from meat by salting. The superstition
evolved into a myth perpetuated by the Greek empire at a time
when there was considerable tension between Jews and the
Greek governors of large parts of what is now the Middle East.
Along with Christianity, it made its way into Europe, and by
the Middle Ages it had become firmly rooted.*

*Europe's first clear case of blood libel against Jews was in
England in 1144. But it quickly spread throughout Europe
where the Middle Ages and early modern times saw numerous
trials and massacres of Jews as a result. An integral part of
European lore, it was used also by the Nazis.*

France's first blood libel occurred in Blois in 1171. Though no
body was ever found, local Jews were accused all the same of murdering a Christian, and thirty-one men, women, and children
were burned at the stake following a show trial. As if to capitalize
on this horrific trend, similar accusations were soon made in Pon-
toise, Epernay, and Joinville. King Louis VII didn't believe the
charges, but in spite of his statements to that effect to the Jewish
leadership, outbreaks were many, and popular belief in the blood
libel continued.

Although King Louis VII seemed somewhat open-minded at least where blood libel was concerned; his successor, Philippe-Auguste (1180–1223), was anything but. His hatred of Jews had been nurtured since childhood. Shortly after he became king he threw the wealthy Jews of Paris in prison and held them for a huge ransom. The following year, the paid ransom notwithstanding, he banished all the Jews from France and confiscated their property for good measure. So began a relationship between the king and the Jews that was to see a series of expulsions and repatriations throughout his entire reign.

At the time, the kingdom of France did not extend much beyond the borders of the city of Paris, and the Paris of the twelfth century was not the Paris we know today. Philippe-Auguste's wall stopped just north of today's 2nd arrondissement on the right bank of the Seine and ran along part of the present rue Tiquetonne.[1] As a result, the number of Jews actually affected was relatively small. So the neighboring provinces and lands where the king lacked authority frequently became places of refuge. But Philippe-Auguste was undaunted by such minor details as royal authority and jurisdiction, and he frequently pursued his expelled Jews to other territories.

As much as the king despised the Jews, he despised his perpetually barren royal coffers even more, and whenever he needed money for one pet project or another he invited the Jews back so he could extort more money from them. And so it went throughout Philippe-Auguste's reign.

The Jews of France came through the Third Crusade (1189–92) relatively unscathed, though the same could not be said for their brethren in England. But soon after, the bloody Albigensian War in southern France took a grave toll on local Jews, especially in Béziers in 1209. The Albigenses were Christian heretics who were popularly, though incorrectly, believed to have been influenced by Jewish beliefs. (See chapter 8.) Despite papal opposition, they persisted in their beliefs. Pope Innocent III declared a crusade against them in 1208, and Pope Gregory IX established an inquisition in 1233 to put a stop to them. (An inquisition is a council set up by the Roman Catholic Church to crush heresy. There have been many throughout history. The notorious Spanish Inquisition, however, was set up by the Spanish monarchy in 1478 to punish Jews and Muslims who converted to Christianity but continued to practice Judaism or Islam in secret.)

The Jewish survivors of that bloodbath found refuge on the other side of the Pyrenees where they reestablished their community in Gerona, Spain. Of course, refuge is a relative concept, but the Jews would enjoy some safety in Spain, at least for the next 283 years, until they were expelled at the hands of the Spanish Inquisition in 1492.

Though in earlier centuries there were periods when Jews were well integrated into the local economy, increased restrictions on their economic activity mirrored the desire of the Church to constrain what they perceived as Jewish influence on Christian society. Throughout much of French history (as well as the history of the rest of Europe) very few commercial activities were open to Jews, and Jews were also prohibited from owning land. Starting in the twelfth century, money lending became a major source of income for individual Jews and for the community that was dependent on them to run its various institutions. Money lending in this sense refers to private, usually collateral loans (i.e., pawnbroking) at high rates of interest. This was especially true in the parts of France where Jews were expelled and later readmitted.

This method of earning a living came about because both Jews and Christians are forbidden to lend money at interest within their own religious groups; that is, Jews are forbidden to charge interest to other Jews and Christians to other Christians, but neither is forbidden from charging interest to someone outside the group. That situation allowed Jews to earn a living when no other path was open to them, and like many other differences in religious law and practice, it was a source of social and political friction. In the parts of France where commercial regulations were more liberal, Jews were physicians, traders in livestock and agricultural products, and petty government officials.

Money Lending

According to the Torah, Jews are forbidden to lend money at interest to other Jews, and there are a number of interpretations of the Torah's wording that go so far as to eschew the taking of interest from anyone. Likewise, the Roman Catholic Church was opposed to the charging of interest in any form. Nonetheless, when merchants, governments, and individuals were in need of funds and they had none of their own, they borrowed from the wealthy, who loaned money at interest. Jews were not the only people in the money-lending business; this type of commerce crossed religious lines despite the Church's stand against it. Money could be borrowed from priests, merchants, landowners, and even the pope. In much of Europe, Italian merchants like the Lombards, the Medici, and the Caursini competed with Jews in the lending of money at interest.

In the Middle Ages, money lending became a critical source of Jewish income because Jews were excluded from virtually every other occupation. In some cases they were specifically limited to earning a living by lending money, and the interest rates they could charge were strictly regulated. Indeed, interest charged by non-Jewish lenders was much higher. So this raises the question, Just who did run the money-lending business? Was it Jews, or was it the governments that regulated them and whose income was dependent on the derived tax income?

In its effort to contain Jewish participation in day-to-day social and economic life, the Church set up legislative councils. These had a tremendous effect on the daily lives of Jews. One such group, the Fourth Lateran Council (1215), mandated the wearing of a Jewish badge. This was first imposed in Languedoc, Normandy, and Provence. Later, in 1294, the council passed laws prohibiting Jews from residing outside specific Jewish sections of a city or town. The measures extended to legal matters as well. A guardian, or magister Judaeorum, had to be appointed in all lawsuits in which one party was Jewish. Even internal Jewish matters were adjudicated in special public tribunals rather than within the Jewish community. Jews who were witnesses at a trial were forced to take a special oath known as the More Judaico.

More Judaico

Special oaths were required of Jews in legal dealings with Christians. The wording of the oath was intended to humiliate, curse, and imply the inherent untrustworthiness of Jews. Those who devised these oaths structured and composed them to parody actual Jewish oaths that had a basis in Jewish law. The phrasing combined with the rituals performed during its administration involved the imposition of various curses that would be suffered if the oath were broken, and they almost always invoked the name of G-d. It was believed that this would force Jews not to violate the oath.

Such oaths were common throughout Europe from the Middle Ages through the eighteenth century—in France they were used until the mid-nineteenth century—and were administered in the synagogue, just outside the synagogue, or occasionally inside a courtroom. The ritual surrounding the administration of the oath varied from location to location. In some places, simply placing one's hand on the Jewish Bible was enough. In other places, the practice took on bizarre overtones such as forcing the Jew to stand on the skin of a pig or on the skin of a female animal that had given birth the previous night. Frequently the ritual was more important than the actual oath.

This example of a Jewish oath is from Germany in the thirteenth century.[2]

*About the goods for which this man sues against thee, that
thou dost not know of them nor have them, nor hast
taken them into thy possession, neither thyself nor thy
servants . . .*

*So help thee God, who created heaven and earth, valleys
and mountains, wood, foliage, and grass that was not
before;*

*So help thee the Law that God wrote with His hand and
gave to Moses on Mount Sinai; . . . And that so [if] thou
eatest something, thou will become defiled all over, as
did the King of Babylon; And that sulphur and pitch
rain upon thy neck, as it rained upon Sodom and
Gomorrah;*

*And that the earth swallow thee as it did Dathan and Abi-
ram; So art thou true and right.*

And so help thee Adonai; art true in what thou has sworn.

*And so that thou wouldst become leprous like Naaman: it
is true.*

*And so that the blood and the curse ever remain upon thee
which thy kindred wrought upon themselves when they
tortured Jesus Christ and spake thus: His blood be upon
us and upon our children: it is true.*

So help thee God, who appeared to Moses in a burning bush.

It is true the oath thou hast sworn:

*By the soul which on doomsday thou must bring to judg-
ment.*

*Per deum Abraham, per deum Isaac, per deum Jacob it is
true.*

So help thee God and the oath which thou hast sworn.

Amen.

During this same period, Louis IX (1226–70), who was no
fonder of Jews than was Philippe-Auguste, oversaw additional
vicious anti-Jewish measures along with his neighbors, the rulers

of Brittany, Anjou, and Poitou. Louis IX had given the control of several of his provinces to his brother Alphonse of Poitiers. It is difficult to tell which of the brothers was best and most unmerciful at extorting money from his Jewish subjects. Alphonse's preferred method was to jail the Jews under his dominion and then confiscate their possessions while they were in prison.

During this same period an infamous "trial of the Talmud" was held in Paris. It was hardly a trial, however; the texts of the Talmud themselves were the defendants in a sham trial, the verdict of which was predetermined by Pope Gregory IX in his 1239 bull. The sentence was destruction of the Talmud by burning, which was carried out in 1242. (For further discussion see the Paris chapter.)

Louis IX's successors continued his harsh treatment of the Jews. Philip III, known as the Bold, issued an edict forbidding Jews from living in rural localities. His successor, Philip IV (the Fair), in 1285 was sovereign over a country that saw horrific massacres (Troyes, 1285) sparked by yet another blood libel, burning of Jewish leaders at the stake, and edicts prohibiting Jews who were expelled from England from settling in France.

Along with imprisonment, confiscation of property, and expulsion, the Jews of France had to endure numerous accusations of a specifically religious nature. One of these involved desecration of the Host, which, according to Catholic theology, is the representation of the body of Jesus during the Mass. It was widely believed and perpetuated by the Church that Jews, as the rejecters of Jesus' divinity, deliberately desecrated the Host as part of their struggle against Christianity. This was the backdrop for the first trials and executions of Jews in Paris in 1290. (See Paris chapter.)

But apart from the substantial religious differences between the Catholic kings of France and their Jewish subjects, it was the Crown's constant need for money that drove much of the persecution and expulsion. Jewish property could be appropriated for whichever war or building project the king fancied instead of raising taxes on the entire population, causing civil unrest. Of course it goes without saying that it was precisely the fact that Jews were outside the religious and therefore social mainstream that led some of them into the professions that allowed them to accumulate wealth in the first place. However, although a few Jews became rich by lending money at interest, the vast majority of Jews did not earn a great living and many subsisted as best they could within the constraints placed upon them by Christian society.

The seizure of Jewish property and wealth by the French Crown did not always go uncontested. Philip the Fair, in addition to being unfair to the Jews under his control, was unfair in other ways to the lords in the neighboring and far-flung provinces that received the Jews he expelled. He insisted that confiscated Jewish resources remain his, and he would not share the loot with them. It made for difficult relations between France and its neighbors. To add insult to injury, on the occasions the Jews were permitted to resettle in lands under French control, Philip the Fair forced them to participate in the collection of their own property that had been seized prior to their expulsion.

Philip IV's son and heir, Louis X (1314–16), set the stage for a twelve-year return of the Jews his father threw out, but Philip V (1316–22) got rid of them again in 1322 on the heels of massacres in places like Toulouse, Tours, Chinon, and Bourges. In addition, a huge fine was imposed on all French Jewry, and the Crown took the property of the massacred Jews.

When the Black Death spread across Europe, Jews were blamed for it. As a result, a frantic public—egged on by an ever-obliging clergy—massacred Jews all over France in the hope of exorcising the plague from their midst. In 1348, Jews were murdered in Alsace, Provence, Savoy, Dauphiné, and Franche-Comté. At the intervention of the popes of Avignon, the Jews of the city of Avignon and the surrounding communities of Comtat Venaissin region (see Provence) escaped the fate of their brethren. (See later in this section for further discussion.) Jewish blame for the Black Death was to have consequences far beyond the thousands massacred during its scourge. It was to solidify in the minds of Europeans their already detestable image of the Jew, an image that would come to characterize modern anti-Semitism.

The plague notwithstanding, money once again proved to be as good a reason as any for Jewish resettlement. Under Charles V (1364–80), the Jews were authorized to return to France for a period of twenty years so that the taxes collected from them could be used to ransom the king's father, John II, from prison in England.

That twenty-year period was later extended another six years and then another ten in 1374. But the new king, Charles VI (1380–1422), declined to agree to the years added to the original twenty, and in 1394 he decreed that the following year Jews had to get out of France altogether, even in those areas where they were living under the unratified decree extension.

Prior to the expulsion, Charles VI presided over violent oppression that took place all over his kingdom, particularly in Paris and Nantes. Massacres, persecution, and expulsion continued through the fifteenth century, and by the beginning of the sixteenth century the only Jews left in what we know today as France were in Alsace, Lorraine, Avignon and Comtat Venaissin, and Nice.

Of course, France was not the only country in which Jews were persecuted; far from it. And the sixteenth century saw immigration into southwest France from Spain and Portugal by so-called New Christians. New Christians were in reality Jews or descendants of Jews who had been forced to convert during the Spanish Inquisition. Known as Conversos or derisively as Marranos, Alboraycos, or Tornadizos,[3] they frequently practiced Judaism in secret or maintained vestiges of Jewish practice for many generations.

In 1550, Henry II granted a group of New Christians (who were in reality secret Jews) the right to settle in France. They settled in the southwest in Bordeaux, in and around Bayonne, and later in the nearby towns of Peyrehorade, Bidache, Labastide-Clairence, La Rochelle, Nantes, and Rouen. Some but not all of the settlers were in fact Conversos. Fearful of being found out, the Conversos' public lives were Christian and they continued to maintain their Spanish culture and language. But even that proved to be a double-edged sword because, as Spaniards, they were suspected of being loyal to Spain and of conspiring to deliver the town over to the Spanish king. In 1625, in reprisal for this perceived treason, their property was confiscated and tax imposed as compensation and in exchange for a new settlement permit. The new permit recognized the Conversos as Jews, but it did not grant them the right to practice Judaism.

One of the few regions where Jews enjoyed relative safety was in Comtat Venaissin, in what is now Provence. There, under the protection of the popes of Avignon—during the era when the papacy was located in Avignon and not in Rome—Jews flourished. But even that area was not trouble-free and expulsions did occur. In the end, Jews were only permitted to live in the cities of Avignon, Carpentras, Cavaillon, and L'Isle-sur-la-Sorgue. (See the Comtat Venaissin section in chapter 9 for more on this.)

The Thirty Years' War ended in 1648 with the Treaty of Westphalia and gave France the towns of Metz and Verdun in what is now Lorraine. Even though an order was in place prohibiting Jews from living in France, Jews were actually encouraged to settle in this region. In fact, Lorraine is the only region of France that has had a Jewish community, albeit small, without interruption. In the city of Metz, for example, the Jewish population went from three families in 1565 to ninety-six families in 1657.

Though it was the first time since 1394 that Jews were legally allowed to live in the French kingdom, life was pretty restricted. For the most part travel outside the province was constrained and many were even forbidden to travel outside the towns in which they lived. Places where Jews could work were similarly limited. Yet despite this, the Jews of Alsace and Lorraine were afforded a good deal of protection and Jews from other parts of Europe arrived as settlers: Charleville took in Jews from Holland, and refugees from the Chmielnicki Cossack massacres in Poland and the Ukraine found refuge there as well. In the south, the duke of Savoy declared Nice and Villefranche-de-Conflent free ports in 1648. Such seeming generosity did not represent a great advance in liberal thinking or religious tolerance; it was merely practical: Jews filled an economic void and the local monarchs were eager to take advantage.

In the seventeenth century, Jews in Comtat Venaissin broadened the scope of their businesses and attempted to settle in Languedoc and Provence. Previously, a Jew could only attend markets and trade fairs in those areas. Fearing competition, the non-Jewish merchants protested and the Jews were forced to leave. Undaunted, and taking their cue from the Conversos who settled in and around Bordeaux, they, along with other Jews from Alsace, began to settle there and take up the textile trade.

Paris was off-limits to Jews for centuries. The various bans and expulsions from France meant that Jews could live in neighboring kingdoms at the sufferance of the local monarch or nobles. Nonetheless, in the early eighteenth century, Jews began to leave the relative hospitality of some areas for the capital. The welcome was not warm. The few privileges Jews had in their home provinces did not follow them to Paris, and the level of animosity was such that if a Jew died in Paris, his estate was forfeited to the Crown, and burial in the capital had to be in secret.

But by the end of the eighteenth century liberal changes were in the air in many parts of the world and France was no different. The French Revolution in 1789 would not only bring about the overthrow of the French monarchy, but it would forever alter the lives and status of the Jews of France.

Beginning in the second half of the eighteenth century, a number of writers and philosophers had begun to ponder the problem of Jews living in their midst. Montesquieu, for example, though not entirely uncritical of Jewish life, argued for a society that was tolerant of all religions. The Jewish leaders of Alsace were eager to see the establishment of civil rights for their community, and one man, Herz Cerf Berr, who would prove pivotal in the struggle, commissioned the translation of works calling for the establishment of civil rights for Jews. The ill-fated King Louis XVI was not deaf to those new ideas, and in 1783 he decreed the abolition of some Jewish taxes.

Liberalism was truly in fashion. In Metz, a member of parliament held a contest asking for suggestions on ways to make the Jews of France more productive to the nation. Then in 1788, the king charged his minister Chrétien-Guillaume de Lamoignon de Malesherbes with the task of developing a system of civil rights for Jews much as he had done earlier with France's beleaguered Protestants.

The French Revolution

SOME FORTY THOUSAND JEWS lived in France by 1789, the year of the start of the French Revolution. They lived either in Paris, Alsace-Lorraine, or southern France. Those in Paris and Alsace-Lorraine spoke Yiddish, the amalgam of Hebrew, German, and other European languages used by German and eastern European Jews, while the southern Jews spoke French. Laws enacted in 1790 and 1791 granted civil rights to Jews and eliminated the ghettos, and it meant that Jews could take an active part in French society without the restrictions and fear of expulsion that had marked their existence in France for so many centuries. But despite this, the Yiddish-speaking Jews were generally more religious and less integrated into French civil life than their French-speaking brethren.

The Reign of Terror (1793–94) was the watershed that changed France forever. The country's religious institutions suffered greatly during this period. Churches and synagogues were closed, and anything to do with religion of any kind was, very definitely, politically incorrect. Though the implementation of Jewish civil rights was welcome, it came at considerable cost.

As a group outside the mainstream of French life, Jews had the advantage of running their own religious life without theological interference. True, they were subject to special taxes, property confiscation, forced baptism, and other demeaning and restrictive laws, but in the realm of the religious they were left pretty much alone. That changed. Along with civil rights came many new responsibilities—no longer Jews in France, they became French Jews.

Under Napoleon Bonaparte this distinction was codified. It was a hard bargain. Napoleon insisted that Jews, in exchange for the rights of other Frenchmen, bear allegiance first to their country and then to their religion. Napoleon was no friend of the Jewish people and he was hostile to Jewish ways and Jewish theology. But his overall political and social aims made him determined to change them enough to bring them into the French mainstream. Napoleon was frustrated that the granting of civil rights to Jews, whom he looked upon as "a nation within a nation," had what he considered disappointing results. For example, money lending (along with the practice of usury) was still a major Jewish occupation, particularly in Alsace, and he wanted that stamped out. Napoleon also had no use for synagogue services, which were much less formal than those we know now; he considered them chaotic.

To facilitate changes in Jewish society, Napoleon convened an Assembly of Jewish Notables on July 26, 1806. The purpose of this was to make sure there was nothing about Jewish law that was inherently incompatible with French civil law. To ascertain this, government officials posed twelve questions. Once Napoleon was satisfied with the answers he convened a Grand Sanhedrin (traditional Jewish law court) made up of forty-five rabbis and twenty-six laymen to codify the religious principles that were based on the notables' answers to the questions. The Sanhedrin met for two months and turned its comments over to the notables, who continued to form the framework of the organization that in 1808 would come to be known as the Consistoire Central des Juifs de France (Central Consistory of French Jews).

The Consistoire, which is still the governing body of French Jewry, provided that each department (French regional designation similar to a state) with more than two thousand Jews have a council made up of a chief rabbi (grand rabbin), one other rabbi, and three laymen elected by the community elders. The central Consistoire would be in Paris, and it would serve as the administrative organization for the entire country and have at its head three chief rabbis and two laymen. In contrast to the funding for other religious bodies, which was provided by the state, the Jewish community itself would provide the financial backing for the Consistoire.

With the establishment of the Consistoire, Judaism was officially recognized as one of France's religions—though the fact that the Jewish community had to fund the Consistoire clearly shows that Judaism was not considered equal to the others. The Consistoire had jurisdiction in Jewish affairs, but practically its authority was limited to religious matters. Under this system, the rabbinate was responsible for teaching Judaism and for promoting compliance with civil law and authority. In addition, prayers for the Emperor's family were to be added to the Jewish liturgy.

Rabbis David Sinzheim, Joshua Benzion Segre, and Abraham Vita Cologna of Mantua, Italy, were the first three chief rabbis of the Consistoire Central. But the three-chief-rabbi Consistoire was short-lived. Segre died shortly after his appointment and was replaced by Emmanuel Deutz, the rabbi of Koblenz, Germany; Sinzheim died in 1812, and Cologna resigned in 1826. Deutz, until his death in 1842, was de facto the sole chief rabbi, and there has been only one chief rabbi ever since.

Emancipation had its downside. Now an official religion, Judaism as an institution had to sublimate its own needs to those of the state, whose declared goal was to make Jews more French and less Jewish. That often meant accepting the negative consequences of new regulations: Debts owed to Jews were canceled; Jews had to obtain a trade license, renewable every year in their department of residence; there were some restrictions on where Jews could live; the practice of paying substitutes to fulfill military requirements was abolished; and the adoption of surnames was mandated.

The cancellation of debts to individual Jews meant that there would be less money with which to run Jewish community organizations such as schools and charities. Charity (*tzedakah* in Hebrew) toward other Jews has its foundations in Jewish law, and as a result it is a long-standing tradition among Jewish communities all over the world, so any reduction in the ability to fulfill those obligations was taken very seriously.

The Jewish community also maintained its own schools. Education in one form or another has long had a pivotal place in Judaism and within the Jewish community. Long before primary education was made compulsory in France in 1882, Jews maintained their own schools in places like Metz, Strasbourg, Colmar, Paris, and Bordeaux that functioned as conduits for Jewish as well as secular study. Strasbourg, Mulhouse, and Paris established technical schools as well. Eventually a system of state schools gained hegemony over the Jewish ones, and in 1905 Jewish schools lost state funding when France separated church from state—by law if not always in fact.

Though Jews were now legally emancipated, the huge, fundamental changes in daily Jewish life that resulted gave rise to a profound internal crisis. And, as is usually the case with the assimilation of a group long outside the mainstream, legal equality did not mean social acceptance.

Civil Rights: A Double-Edged Sword

After Jews were granted civil rights, moved away from ghettos, and were freed from wearing identifying badges or clothing, the nature of anti-Semitism changed. As long as Jews could be easily identified by their clothes, residence, or profession, in addition to their practices, anti-Semitism was mostly confined to the religious arena. However, as Jews became more integrated into society, anti-Semitism moved from the religious to the social and political realms—Jews as contaminators of French life or the French nation, or German life or the German nation, and so on.

In the nineteenth century, around the same time that Jews were settling into the larger societies in which they lived, a number of racial theories developed in which Jews were identified as polluters of the pure European races (i.e., Aryans). These theories gained quite a following in France and were promulgated by such pseudophilosophers as Joseph Arthur, Comte de Gobineau, Houston Stewart Chamberlain, Edmond Picard, and the composer Richard Wagner. The theories formed much of the basis for Nazism, so it was a short walk from the ghettos to the gas chambers.

Accustomed to living in an insular world, many Jews found it difficult to adjust to dealing with the larger society—and to living with one foot in each world. The children of the generation that saw firsthand the French Revolution and the changes brought about by equal civil rights became part of a wave of converts to Christianity, especially among France's leading Jewish families. It seemed that Bonaparte's policy of legal acceptance had succeeded in frenchifying—and Christianizing—many Jews where persecution and forced conversion had failed.

David Drach was the son-in-law of Emmanuel Deutz, the chief rabbi of the Consistoire Central. He had studied for the rabbinate himself and was the director of Paris's Jewish school. Not only did he convert to Christianity, but he became a priest. And he was not alone. Théodore Ratisbonne, the son of the president of the Consistoire of the Lower Rhine (Alsace), converted in secret, became a priest, took the name of Marie-Théodore Ratisbonne, and officiated at the conversion of his younger brother Alphonse. The brothers founded the order of Notre Dame de Sion (Our Lady of Zion), and later the Fathers of Zion, whose mission it was to convert Jews and further understanding between Jews and Christians. The younger Ratisbonne established the Ecce Homo convent in Jerusalem for the Sisters of Zion and spent the rest of his life working to convert Jews and Muslims to Christianity. To their credit, those orders were among the most vocal of Hitler's Catholic opponents and gave shelter and safe passage to Jews in German-occupied countries during World War II.

While Christianization was one blow to the community, another came to its leadership: There was a shortage of rabbis. Prior to the Revolution, the yeshivas around Alsace and Lorraine and in parts of eastern and central Europe trained the rabbis for the Ashkenazi community, particularly the yeshiva in Metz. But when the Metz yeshiva was shut down by the Revolution, there were few new rabbis. The shortage only added to the community's difficulties. In 1829, after many petitions and much cajoling, the Ministry of Religion in Paris agreed to the establishment of a central rabbinical seminary in Metz. The ministry also put France's official rabbis on the same footing as other religious leaders: Salaries would henceforth be paid by the state and not by the Jewish community (but that would change again in 1905 with the separation of church and state). In 1859 the Metz seminary was moved to Paris, where today it still trains many of France's rabbis.

By the middle of the nineteenth century such significant legal strides had been made in the emancipation of Jews that one could almost call it revolutionary. But there were still some barriers left. One was the More Judaico, the Jewish oath. Its demise was initiated by Consistoire Central member Adolphe Crémieux and finally acted upon by the Supreme Court of Appeals in 1846.

Adolphe Crémieux (1796–1880)

Adolphe Crémieux's opposition to the More Judaico was long-standing. His refusal to take the oath himself, which as a lawyer he was required to do to practice in court, was a turning point in its eventual elimination. In addition to his personal fight, he defended others who refused to take the oath, and in 1827 he won two cases brought against Jews who had repudiated it. The More Judaico was taken off the books as a result, and Crémieux gained a reputation as a defender of Jewish rights.

In years to come he would serve in regional Consistoires as well as in the central one in Paris, whose president he became in 1843. During the Damascus Affair (which is discussed later in this section), Crémieux was instrumental, along with England's Moses Montefiore, in securing the release of the Jews held prisoner.

Crémieux was elected to the Chamber of Deputies in 1842 and later, after taking part in the Revolution of 1848, became the minister of justice of the provisional government. Despite his support of the presidency of Louis-Napoleon, his later opposition to Louis-Napoleon's 1851 coup d'état landed him in jail. But by 1869 he was back in the chamber. With the fall of Louis-Napoleon's Second Empire he again became minister of justice, and among other things he promulgated the 1870 Decree Crémieux that granted French citizenship to the Jews of Algeria.

During the years he was out of official politics, Crémieux concentrated on Jewish affairs, becoming president of the Alliance Israélite Universelle in 1864. In that capacity he worked on behalf of oppressed Jews in other parts of the world, particularly in Morocco, Romania, and Russia. He was instrumental in getting charges of blood libel dropped against two Russian Jews, who had been convicted in St. Petersburg of murdering a Christian child.

The Rothschilds

The Rothschilds have been prominent in French finance, arts, letters, and philanthropy since the middle of the nineteenth century. And for some two hundred years, the House of Rothschild, a bank with branches in Europe's financial capitals, has played a major role in the economic history of Europe and indeed the world.

The family came originally from Germany and it takes its name from the red shield that hung in front of the Frankfurt house of Isaac Elhanan, the grandson of a man named Uri, the first recorded Rothschild, who died around 1500. The family continued to use the name though they no longer lived in the house. Some 160 years after the death of Isaac Elhanan, Mayer Amschel Rothschild was born in 1743. At the age of twenty-five Mayer Amschel became a court agent to William IX of Hesse-Kassel, with whom he had done business in antique coins for some years. He gradually built up substantial financial holdings and created a successful business.

James Jacob Rothschild (1792–1868), the youngest son of Mayer Amschel Rothschild, founded the Paris branch of the family business, Rothschild Frères, and was a powerful force in French banking for nearly forty years. He was a leader of the French Jewish community at a time just after civil rights had been granted, and he was a legendary philanthropist. Among his gifts to the city of Paris is the Rothschild Hospital. His wife, Betty, was a patron of the arts and supported writers like Heinrich Heine.

Mayer Amschel's other sons founded other branches of the family business: Nathan Mayer, the London branch; Carl Mayer, the Italian branch; and Salomon Mayer, the Vienna branch. Amschel Mayer remained with the Frankfurt end of the business.

Alphonse Rothschild (1827–1905) and Edmond James Rothschild (1845–1934), James's eldest and youngest sons, carried on the family traditions in both finance and Jewish causes—Alphonse as a banker and philanthropist, and Edmond as a backer of Jewish settlements in Palestine. Another son, Gustave (1829–1911), was president of the Paris Consistoire.

It has been the descendants of James Rothschild who have

led the family in France since the end of World War II: Baron
Guy de Rothschild (1909–), Baron Alain de Rothschild
(1910–82), and Baron Elie Robert de Rothschild (1917–).
The family continues to play a vital role in the life of France, its
Jewish community, and the Jewish community at large. The
government of French President François Mitterand national-
ized the Rothschild bank in 1982.

Until now, much of French Jewry, indeed most Jews all over the world, practiced what we would describe today as Orthodox Judaism—that is, Jewish life built around the Torah, Torah study, Talmudic interpretations of the Torah, family life, daily prayers, and the synagogue. But in the years following emancipation, French Jews were under a lot of pressure to change, both from within their own ranks and from Jews outside France. It was not a coincidence that this pressure followed their entry into main-stream French society, nor was it a trend confined to France: In Germany just across the border, what would come to be known as Reform Judaism was taking shape.

Reform reflected the desire of many Jews to make Judaism look more like the rest of religious society—Christianity—with-out compromising Jewish theology. With this in mind, a reluctant body of France's chief rabbis met in Paris from May 13 to 21, 1856. Their task was to work out some sort of policy to address what was becoming a disturbing trend away from traditional Judaism and in some cases away from Judaism altogether. The Alsatian repre-sentatives were the ones most opposed to any sort of reform, but everyone was determined to avoid a community rift. Sadly, the compromises were nicht a hien und night a hair—a Yiddish phrase that means neither here nor there.

Many of the changes were to synagogue services. The number of pyyutim (liturgical poems added to the regular service, espe-cially on Rosh Hashanah, the New Year) were limited (this also served to shorten some services by quite a bit as the number and length of pyyutim can be considerable). Special services were instituted for the blessing of newborns, something that would look like Christian baptism. That flew in the face of Jewish tradition. According to Jewish law, a male child is circumcised eight days following birth and given a name; female children are named by their parents at the first Torah reading following birth. More ceremonies à la Christianity were added to funeral services, and rabbis began to wear clerical garb similar to that worn by Christian clergy. In addition, services were shortened and sermons were given. The traditional Jewish Sabbath morning service, for example, can be as long as three to four hours; services on Yom Kippur are virtually all day. A confirmation ceremony for girls was also added—what we know as the Bat Mitzvah. In traditional Judaism only boys come of age for religious purposes; at age thirteen they become Bar Mitzvah.

Other controversies arose over the use of an organ during services. According to Jewish law, music must not be played on either the Sabbath or on the festival holy days. But the French rabbinate decided that it was permissible provided a non-Jew played the music. Its use would vary throughout the country, though, and it would be done only at the request of the local rabbi and authorization by the department's chief rabbi.

Even with the Christianizing changes in Jewish ritual and enhanced legal status for Jews, social acceptance was slow and anti-Semitism ran deep in the French heart. Toward the middle of the century, a number of anti-Jewish riots broke out in France as a result of the Damascus Affair. In 1840 Jews in Damascus, Syria, were accused of blood libel by the local Christian Arabs after the disappearance of a Capuchin monk and his servant. Over one hundred Jewish men were sent to prison and tortured, including some prominent local Jews. The French consul supported the charge against the Jews. Because the French government backed Mehmet Ali, the Egyptian ruler of Syria, the consul's word could not be ignored. So the powerless Jews of Damascus sought help from their French and British brethren. Help came in the persons of Great Britain's Sir Moses Montefiore and Adolphe

Crémieux, vice president of the Consistoire Central. Though the Damascus Jews were released, the event had a serious impact on the Jews of France. Jews, mainly in Alsace, were attacked and their houses and property were damaged. Eventually the army had to be called in to restore order.

The Damascus Affair was not the only incident that underscored the need for Jewish self-protection. In 1858 six-year-old Edgardo Mortara, an Italian Jew, was forcibly taken from his parents by the papal police. Edgar had been seriously ill, and the family's fourteen-year-old Catholic maid, fearing he would die, had him secretly baptized. The Church insisted the child was now a Catholic and could not be raised by his Jewish parents. The Church wouldn't budge. No protest moved it, not even the intervention of Louis-Napoleon. Mortara was raised in a Catholic institution under Vatican guardianship and never returned to his family. Eventually he became a priest."[4]

Nearly 150 years later, the Jewish community's bitterness over that assault on Judaism and parenthood once again came to the surface when Pope John Paul II beatified Pope Pius IX in September 2000. Pius IX, who oversaw young Mortara's kidnapping and his subsequent Catholic education, upheld the laws requiring Jews in Italy to live in ghettos, opposed religious tolerance, and referred to Jews as dogs. Similar custody situations would attain even greater significance during and after the Shoah. (See chapter 10 for more details.)

The election to the presidency and subsequent imperial accession of Louis-Napoleon (Napoleon III) in 1852 brought renewed fears that some of the discriminatory acts introduced by his uncle (Napoleon Bonaparte) would once again be put into practice. But the Second Empire (1852–1870) turned out to be a period of relative calm. Though anti-Semitism was by no means dead, and influential Catholic groups still stood in the way of Jewish progress in places like universities, Jews were making their way up the social, cultural, and political ladder. Achille Fould was the first Jewish member of the Chamber of Deputies (1834), and Adolphe

Crémieux followed him; Jacques Halévy was elected to the Academy of Fine Arts; and Rachel (the stage name of Eliza Rachel Félix) was one of France's most popular actresses. During this time, the Rothschild family became leaders in business and industry.

Though the middle of the nineteenth century was a fairly good time for the Jews of France, the political upheavals wrought by the Franco-Prussian War (1870–71) would have far-reaching consequences for both France and her Jewish citizens. France's humiliating defeat in 1871 created new problems when Alsace and part of Lorraine, long the heart of French Jewry, were lost to Germany. The Jews living in those provinces had to decide whether to remain French or to become German. Those who chose to remain French had to be integrated into French and Jewish society in other locations. As a result of immigration to other parts of France, new Consistoires were created in the cities of Vesoul, Lille, and Besançon.

The rise of the French Third Republic (1870–1940) saw an increase in anti-Semitism—this time fomented by royalists and clergy as a political device to divert attention away from societal demands for reform following France's defeat. Anti-Semitic newspapers were abundant on the right and left, and groups like the Assumptionists, along with socialists like Charles Fourier and Pierre-Joseph Proudhon, tried to prove that the Jews and the Freemasons started the French Revolution. Jews were also blamed for the collapse of the Union Générale, a Catholic bank. In the Chamber of Deputies in 1891, no fewer than thirty-two members demanded that the Jews be expelled (yet again) from France.

Few anti-Semitic enterprises were as extensive as that of Edouard Drumont. In 1885 he published the best-selling book *La France Juive (Jewish France)*, a diatribe in which he claimed that France was being taken over by an alien culture—that of the bloodsucking Jew. Later, in 1889, Drumont formed the French National Anti-Semitic League, and in 1892, with support from the Catholic Church, he launched his newspaper *La Libre Parole* (the *Free Word*—*free* meaning free of Jewish taint or control), in which, among other things, he zealously accused Jews in the army of selling out France in the Franco-Prussian war. *La France Juive* sold some 150,000 copies during its first two years in print, and remained in print well into the twentieth century.

But Jews had become firmly entrenched in French society. By the second half of the nineteenth century, Jews could be found in virtually every profession. And by the eve of World War I, Paris had been made the art center of the world by Jewish artists like Pissarro, Soutine, Chagall, and Modigliani; Sarah Bernhardt was the toast of French theater (she eventually converted to Christianity); and Jews gave French literature and philosophy the work of Adolphe Franck, Henri Bergson, Emile Durkheim, Marcel Proust, and André Maurois.

In 1889, French Jews celebrated the centennial of the Revolution with their fellow Frenchmen. Jews had indeed come a long way in the past one hundred years, but during the next two decades the fate of one man would become inextricably linked with that of France's Jews, and it would betray a nasty truth exemplified by the French expression *plus ça change, plus c'est la même chose* (the more things change, the more they remain the same).

The Dreyfus Affair

ON OCTOBER 15, 1894, Alfred Dreyfus, a captain on the French army general staff, was arrested and accused of selling artillery secrets to the Germans.

Dreyfus was born in Mulhouse, in Alsace, in what was at the time of his arrest the French territory that had been annexed by Germany following the Franco-Prussian war. From a well-to-do and prominent upper-middle-class Jewish family, he was educated in Paris and later graduated near the top of his class at the Ecole Supérieure de Guerre (War College). He was the only Jew appointed to the French army general staff, and he settled into a comfortable life in a fashionable Paris district with his wife and soon their two children.

The accusation of treason was brought in 1894. The evidence against Dreyfus had been forged by a cadre of anti-Semitic officers who manipulated the anti-German paranoia of the French army and fabricated a case against the one staff member they could get away with making the scapegoat—the Jew. The real spy was Major Ferdinand Walsin Esterhazy. Major Hubert Henry and others colluded with many in the army and the government, including the minister of war, and engineered a conspiracy so insidious that the fallout from it ripped France asunder and threatened to bring down the Republic itself.

Following a show trial, in which Dreyfus was found guilty, and a public degradation ceremony, in which he was stripped of his rank and his military insignias, Dreyfus was given a life sentence and sent to the notorious Devil's Island prison in French Guiana.

One of the reporters covering the degradation ceremony was Theodor Herzl of the Viennese *Neue Freie Presse*. The cries of "death to the Jews" emanating with such vehemence from a crowd in what was supposedly one of the most enlightened societies in Europe had a profound effect on Herzl. It was as a direct result of that trial that he wrote *Der Judenstaat (The Jewish State)*, which was to form the philosophical basis for modern political Zionism.

By 1897, there were only a handful of people in France who were convinced of Dreyfus's innocence—his family among them—and they were dedicated to reversing the gross miscarriage of justice. Intense legal battles, in which evidence and information were deliberately withheld from the Dreyfus camp, followed his conviction and imprisonment. Eventually, some very influential writers and politicians (known as Dreyfusards), determined to see the verdict reversed, spoke out against the army and the government. Among them were Léon Blum, Lucien Herr, Georges Clemenceau, and Emile Zola. It was Zola's "J'Accuse" (I Accuse), an open letter to the president of the Republic, Félix Faure, that

"J'Accuse" by Emile Zola in *L'Aurore*

finally won Dreyfus a new trial. But it wasn't until 1906 (after three trials and the fall of the government) that the verdict was overturned. Dreyfus was reinstated into the army and promoted to the rank of major.

In 1995, one hundred years after Dreyfus's arrest, some seventeen hundred invited guests of the Consistoire Central heard General Jean-Louis Mourrut, head of the army's historical service, finally and officially admit that the evidence against Captain Alfred Dreyfus had been fabricated. His appearance was prompted by a 1994 article in the army historical journal that questioned Dreyfus's innocence by suggesting that it was merely the position generally accepted by historians. The outcry in the French Jewish community was such that Mourrut's predecessor was fired.

The separation of church and state in France came as a direct result of the Dreyfus affair. Judaism, along with France's other religions, no longer had official status or government financial support of its religious schools and other institutions. With the cessation of state support, the Consistoire found itself in disarray. In the midst of this came the death of the country's chief rabbi, Zadoc Kahn, who had been a major figure in the French Jewish community ever since his election as chief rabbi of Paris in 1869. The resultant reorganization of the Consistoire turned it into a kind of federal system of local Jewish communities with some centralized services such as the chief rabbinate and the rabbinical seminary.

The first years of the twentieth century saw a number of demographic changes in France's Jewish population. Between 1881 and 1914, the upheaval in eastern Europe led some twenty-five thousand Jews to immigrate to France from Russia, Poland, and Romania, and also from the Ottoman Empire—Salonika, Constantinople (now Istanbul), and Smyrna. But this immigration stopped when the Great War (World War I) broke out in 1914.

With a new war to fight against Germany, internal hatreds were put on the back burner, at least temporarily, for the good of the nation. Anti-Semitic campaigns stopped and Jews and Christians banded together in a Union Sacrée (sacred union) or common front. Germany's defeat in 1918 and the restoration of Alsace and Lorraine to France also meant the reunification of Jews with a region that had been an integral part of their lives for hundreds of years.

The defeat of the Ottoman Empire opened the floodgates, and more immigrants from Turkey and Greece came to Paris and to large southern cities. In addition, vicious pogroms in the Ukraine and Poland brought Jewish refugees to France. When immigration to the United States was put on a quota system in 1924, many Jews who might have gone to North America went instead to France. France was often used as a transit point after 1933 for Jews on their way to the United States or to Palestine.

In the years between the two world wars, American expatriates went to Paris to write, paint, and develop the art and philosophy that would characterize much of the twentieth century, while the Jews of France debated the merits of political Zionism—the movement to redevelop a Jewish homeland in Palestine. At the same time, they continued to assimilate, or so they thought. Though not completely out of the picture, Jewish studies declined in importance. In 1936 Léon Blum became the first Jewish prime minister of France, but by then, Germany had risen from the ashes and had begun again to prepare for war. For the third time in seventy years, France, and France's Jews, would come up against the enemy on their eastern border. This confrontation would bring horrors heretofore unimaginable, even in wartime.

World War II

*H*ITLER AND THE GERMANS made no secret of their animosity toward France. It was payback time for the humiliation of 1918 and the Treaty of Versailles. The Germans invaded France on May 10, 1940—just ten months after their September 1, 1939, invasion of Poland that was the start of World War II. On June 14, Paris capitulated. Before the month was out an armistice dividing France into an occupied and an unoccupied zone was concluded. The occupied zone in the north was governed directly by the German military; the unoccupied zone was governed by the collaborationist French government headquartered in Vichy under Philippe Pétain; and Alsace-Lorraine was annexed to the Third Reich. At the time, it is estimated that three hundred thousand Jews lived in France, but that is just an educated guess because Jews in France were no longer required to identify themselves as Jews for official purposes.

Beginning in September 1940 and ending in July 1942, anti-Jewish laws were instituted throughout the country. Each subsequent law was more restrictive than the previous one, so that by

July 1942 everything had been put in place for the French phase of the Final Solution to the Jewish Question in Europe (Hitler's decision to exterminate the Jews).

- September 27, 1940—order for a Jewish census
- October 4, 1940—order from the Vichy government to revise the status of Jews, dividing them into French Jews—Jews who had been or whose families had been in France for generations—and newcomers, refugees, and so on
- October 18, 1940—law requiring the registration of Jewish businesses and the appointment of administrators over them
- April 26, 1941—the category of Jew extended to include those of Jewish descent who were not Jews; they too were forbidden to take part in the economic activities now barred to Jews
- May 28, 1941—Jewish-owned capital forbidden to circulate in business transactions
- August 13, 1941—radios in Jewish possession confiscated
- September 28, 1941—Jews could not keep proceeds from the forced sale of their property
- December 14, 1941—a fine of one billion francs levied on the Jewish community; fifty-three Jewish members of the Resistance executed; eleven hundred Jews deported
- February 7, 1942—Jews subject to a curfew from 8 P.M. to 6 A.M. and forbidden to change residence
- March 24, 1942—definition of Jews expanded
- May 29, 1942—Jews required to wear a yellow badge: a star of David with the word *Juif* in the center
- July 8, 1942—Jews prohibited from using public parks, squares, gardens, and sports facilities, and limited to one hour per day to go food shopping[5]

Though these laws were on the books in all of France, they were only binding in the occupied zone in the north, and this did not change even after all of France became occupied. Laws enacted by the Vichy regime, however, such as the Juif (Jew) stamp on identity cards, were valid throughout both unoccupied and occupied France.

The German bureaucratic apparatus set up throughout the Third Reich for the roundup of Jews and their transfer first to transit camps and then to the Reich's murder centers was superimposed on France. The Vichy authorities collaborated with the Germans on their Jewish policy, but on the whole, a French Jew was luckier to find himself in the Vichy zone than in the occupied zone. The so-called foreign Jews, however, were subjected to the same level of anti-Jewish measures in the Vichy zone as Jews in occupied France, and they were in as much danger of being sent east (usually to Poland) to a concentration camp.

Caving in to German pressure, the Vichy government set up the Commissariat Général aux Questions Juives (General Commission on Jewish Questions) under the supervision of Xavier Vallat. This right-wing member of the French parliament blamed France's problems on the Jews, including the rise of the Third Republic and the institution of democracy. But Vallat was a veteran of the Great War and a loyal member of a veterans' organization, albeit a right-wing one. Therein lay his primary loyalty—to France and to the army, not to Germany. Jewish veterans found an unlikely friend in Vallat. But the Germans, wary of Vallat's allegiances, replaced him after a year with Louis Darquier de Pellepoix. Not only was de Pellepoix a vicious anti-Semite, but rumor had it he had been a German agent for years.

French soil harbored a number of concentration camps. Foreign Jews were sent mainly to Pithiviers and Beaune-la-Rolande. There was a smaller camp at Compiègne, and some Jews were deported from places like Angers, Lyon, and Toulouse. The partially completed housing development in Drancy, a suburb of Paris, was converted into the main transit camp. The internees lived there in unsanitary, disease-ridden conditions before they were shipped to Auschwitz, near Kraków, Poland. Very few returned at war's end.

The concentration camp Natzweiler-Struthof in Alsace (see the chapter on Alsace-Lorraine, chapter 14, for more information) was mainly for political prisoners. In 1944, with the approach of the Allied armies, the inmates were sent to Dachau in Germany. Natzweiler-Struthof had the distinction of providing the Reich University in Strasbourg with human subjects for its lethal medical experiments. Some one hundred Jewish prisoners, sent from Auschwitz especially so they could become racial anthropology museum pieces, were gassed there.

Waves of roundups began on March 27, 1942. One of the main ones, part of the second wave, took place in Paris from July 16 to 17, 1942: Some thirteen thousand men, women, and children were arrested and sent to Auschwitz via Drancy. In the unoccupied zone, the Vichy police did their part in the deportation of the foreign Jews. In one mass arrest on August 15, 1942, over seven thousand Jews, mainly refugees from Belgium, Holland, and Germany, were turned over to the Germans. Those Jews had sought refuge in French cities with large Jewish populations—Toulouse, Marseille, Lyon, and Nice. The third and fourth waves came in the spring and fall of 1943—the third in Marseille and the fourth in the former Italian zone (in southeastern France) where a number of Jews had taken refuge. Of Nice's twenty-five thousand Jews, six thousand were deported.

The Postwar Years to the Present

*F*RANCE'S JEWISH COMMUNITY was devastated during the occupation and the war. Only about 180,000 people, out of a prewar population of 300,000, survived the Shoah.

Community organizations were in disarray and morale was low. The complicity of the French government in German murder and other atrocities was betrayal for Jews who had considered themselves Frenchmen and who had expected that the French government would protect them along with its other citizens. It proved to be a turning point for French Jewry. They would hereafter take a more self-protective stand on many future issues, even to the point of being at odds with their government.

The postwar population was an admixture of established French Jewish families and immigrants from central and eastern Europe. By 1951, the population had grown to 250,000. The migration of North African Jews from Egypt, Morocco, Tunisia, and Algeria between 1954 and 1961 boosted the population by another 100,000, and Algerian independence in 1962 saw it increase yet again. Of Algeria's 110,000 Jews, virtually all had moved to France proper by 1963. Moroccan and Tunisian Jews followed them throughout the 1960s. This was particularly true after the 1967 Arab-Israeli War. By 1970, the Jewish community of France had changed, irrevocably, from Ashkenazic to Sephardic. The influx of North African Jews and their integration into the French economy resulted in new Jewish communities throughout France and the revitalization of dormant Jewish communities, particularly in the south. Today, more than half the Jews in France live in and around Paris. Marseille is the second largest Jewish community; there are sizable communities in Montpellier, Toulouse, Nice, Lyon, Grenoble, and Strasbourg. However, Strasbourg remains predominantly Ashkenazic. The current Jewish population is around 800,000— the largest in Europe and the second largest Diaspora community (the United States has the largest).

France took many decades to come to grips with its participation in the war against the Jews. They even went so far as to ban some of the films that spoke to the issue of French complicity. One film was *Nuit et Brouillard (Night and Fog,* 1955). In this documentary about Nazi concentration camps, filmmaker Alain Resnais depicted the Shoah's horrors using the commentary of a former camp inmate, Jean Cayrol. In it he juxtaposed black-and-white film of the camp with latter-day color shots. The film contained references to French collusion in the deportation of Jews from France and was banned by the government until those references were deleted.

It was not only French participation in persecutions of Jews that the government didn't want exposed. The general subject of collaboration—Frenchman against Frenchman—was taboo until fairly recently. Films like Marcel Ophuls's 1970 *The Sorrow and the Pity,* along with *Hotel Terminus,* his film about Klaus Barbie, or *Chantons sous l'Occupation,* the 1976 film by André Halimi about the role of France's entertainers during the war, were highly criticized in France. It wasn't until 1995, when President Jacques Chirac spoke at the newly inaugurated memorial to the victims of the 1942 Vélodrome d'Hiver (winter bicycle stadium) roundup (see Paris chapter), that France publicly acknowledged what it and its citizens had done to other French citizens during World War II.

Between the end of World War II and the long-delayed French admissions of responsibility for some of the events of the war, there were other times when French Jewry's interests were at odds with that of the government.

Trouble arose during the 1973 Six-Day War between Israel and the Arab states. President Charles de Gaulle took an anti-Israel position, and French politics bristled with anti-Israel and anti-Semitic (disguised as anti-Zionist) propaganda. The Jewish community was subject to a great deal of pressure to denounce Israel, and thinly veiled threats were common. But French Jewry stood firm in its support for Israel and refused to be intimidated. The French Jewish community took solace from the support of many non-Jewish Frenchmen who did not forget that France and Israel had been strong friends for many years.

In September 1997 the Roman Catholic Church in France issued an unprecedented statement apologizing for its silence during the persecution and deportation of Jews in World War II. The French Episcopal Committee for Relations with Judaism

Poster announcing demonstration against the
United Nations for its vote equating Zionism
with racism

explained that the statement would deal with "the question of the silence of the church and its pastors between 1940 and 1942," when the anti-Jewish legislation was put in place, but that it would not go into the actions of individual Church leaders during the period.

Although during the war the Church initially acquiesced to Vichy's anti-Jewish measures, and some of its leaders hailed Marshal Philippe Pétain, the head of the Vichy government, as the savior of France, a reaction set in after the massive roundup of Jews by French police in Paris on July 16, 1942 (see the 15th Arrondissement section of the Paris chapter). Some bishops, including Jules Salieges of Toulouse and Cardinal Pierre Gerlier of Lyon, expressed open opposition to the Vichy regime.

After the war, one hundred priests in their prison clothes celebrated Mass in Paris for concentration camp victims and their families. But General Charles de Gaulle refused to meet the archbishop of Paris, Cardinal Emmanuel Suhard, and pleaded with Pope Pius XII to remove his Paris nuncio, Valerio Valeri, on the grounds that both men had collaborated with the Nazis.

Father Valeri was soon replaced, however, by Angelo Roncalli, the future Pope John XXIII, who sought to heal the deep divisions in the Church. At war's end, reconciliation meetings were held between Catholics and Jews, and committees and organizations were set up to improve relations.

But a number of wartime collaborators enjoyed the protection of the Catholic Church. Among them was Paul Touvier. Touvier, a high official in Lyon working for the Vichy regime, was also an aide to Lyon's Gestapo chief Klaus Barbie, known as the "Butcher of Lyon" for his cruelty. In June 1944 seven Jews were executed on Touvier's orders as reprisal for the murder by the French Resistance of Philippe Henriot, Vichy's propaganda chief. After the war Touvier became a fugitive and was tried and convicted twice in absentia. In 1971 President Georges Pompidou pardoned him after Church officials intervened. But when Jewish survivors and French Resistance groups collected new evidence against him he again went into hiding. He moved from monastery to monastery until he was arrested in 1989 in a Catholic priory in Nice. Sentenced to life in prison in 1994, he died there in 1996.

The Church's 1997 apology came on the fifty-seventh anniversary of the first of a series of anti-Semitic laws passed by the Vichy regime. Not incidentally, it coincided with the opening of the trial of Maurice Papon, the only senior Vichy official to go before a court since the purges immediately after the war. Official documents showed that Mr. Papon (eighty-seven at the time of the trial), who was accused of crimes against humanity, rounded up nearly sixteen hundred Jewish men, women, and children in Bordeaux and sent them to the transit camp at Drancy, and from there they were deported to death camps in Nazi Germany. After the war he had a successful career, becoming chief of police in Paris and budget minister, until the allegations about his wartime role surfaced in 1980.

The six-month trial ended in April 1998. Papon was convicted and sentenced to ten years in prison. The trial received worldwide news coverage and was the talk of France, where opinion was sharply divided. Many believed that after so many years there should have been no trial at all. In October 1999, on the eve of his appeals hearing, Papon escaped to Switzerland. After a terrific hue and cry he was arrested by the Swiss police and sent back to France. In March 2000 President Jacques Chirac turned down Papon's plea for a medical pardon.

It is interesting to note that many of France's wartime secrets are still locked up under a sixty-year gag rule for official documents.

French Jewry Today

*T*ODAY, THE CONSISTOIRE CENTRAL de France is the official representative of French Jewry. Under its auspices, rabbis are trained and appointed, kashrus is supervised, children are educated, and religious law is administered. The Consistoire is primarily orthodox and Ashkenazic in orientation. As a result, other organizations were established to meet other needs, such as the Union Libérale Israélite, which trained its rabbis at the Institut International d'Etudes Hébraïques, and also a number of independent organizations serving the Sephardic and Hasidic communities.

As in most countries, many of France's Jews either are nonobservant or they observe very little. But there are hundreds of cultural, social, and political organizations around which Jews maintain some ties to the community, even if those ties are not specifically religious in nature. In 1944, the Conseil Représentatif des Israélites de France (CRIF) was founded as a means to coordinate the many disparate groups that had formed and were continuing to form.

By the early 1980s the character of Jewish leadership had begun to change from Ashkenazic to Sephardic, and it was also becoming more, not less, Orthodox. Many Jewish leaders were opposed to organizing activities that were strictly secular even within a Jewish context. All of France's chief rabbis since 1981 have been Sephardic. The current chief rabbi, Joseph Sitruk, was reelected to a second seven-year term in June 1994. The community is currently in a bit of flux as the traditionalist leadership jockeys to maintain control over the major French Jewish organizations.

Even today anti-Semitism is still a player in French politics and society. The Front National (the National Front) an ultra-nationalist right-wing party headed by Jean-Marie Le Pen, has found fertile ground with its opposition to immigrants and non-French influences (i.e., Jewish media, Jewish bankers, but also Muslims), a platform that also includes denial of the Shoah. He has made common cause with some of France's establishment right-wing political factions and has considerable support in southern and northern France, particularly in areas of high unemployment and high crime. Some regions have even elected Front National candidates to their municipal and regional governments.

But anti-Jewish sentiment in France doesn't only come from its traditional nest on the extreme right; it also comes from members of France's large Muslim community.

When violence between Israel and the Palestinians escalated radically in the fall of 2000, Jews in Germany, England, Spain, and Belgium became targets of bombings, individual attacks, and demonstrations by Muslims. This was particularly true in France, home to an estimated five million Muslims.

In events reminiscent of the 1930s and 1940s, two synagogues in Paris were firebombed, along with one in Lyon and one in southern France, and Jewish businesses were defaced with anti-Semitic graffiti. A school bus full of Jewish children was stoned by a group of North African men on the outskirts of Paris. The anti-Jewish incidents even extended to non-Jews when a merchant in Strasbourg with a Jewish-sounding name was the victim of an attack. And in Paris, Muslim demonstrators carried banners calling for "death to the Jews." The outcry, both popular and official, against these attacks was immediate and unequivocal, but the fear that has been stirred up cannot be easily assuaged.

Although France's history with its Jewish citizens has been difficult, and difficulties continue to arise, to all intents and purposes France's Jews are indeed both French and Jewish. Jews are completely integrated into French society and can be found in every walk of life. Before World War II, one Jew, Léon Blum, had risen to the office of prime minister; in the postwar era, two Jews, René Mayer and Pierre Mendès France, attained that office.

Despite the troubles, French Jews look to the future with cautious optimism. Though they are ever mindful of the past, particularly the recent past, this is nonetheless one of the largest Jewish communities in the world (nearly 800,000), and an active and thriving one at that. Throughout France one can see the remnants of the Jewish communities of old in street names such as rue de la Juiverie, rue aux Juifs, and avenue de la synagogue. But in many more cities and towns French Jews are alive and well.

CHAPTER TWO

Paris

A Short History of Jews in Paris

THE CITY WE KNOW today as Paris has been inhabited for over two thousand years. It was called Lutetia Parisiorum for the Parisi, a Gallic tribe, who lived surrounded by swampland on what is now the Ile de la Cité. Rome conquered the area in the fourth century C.E., and Jews have lived here ever since.

In the twelfth century, Benjamin of Tudela (in Spain), who traveled all over the known world and chronicled its Jewish communities, called Paris Ha-ir Hagedolah (Hebrew for *that great city*). Despite an often treacherous history for Jews, Paris is certainly a great city and can be appreciated by people of any faith.

Long before Benjamin of Tudela, in the sixth century C.E., the area near the Church of St.-Julien-le-Pauvre (just south of Notre Dame) in the 5th arrondissement was the site of a synagogue. In the tenth and eleventh centuries, a community of Jews lived nearby on the rue de la Harpe between the rue de la Huchette and the rue St.-Séverin. Somewhat later, they lived on a street called the rue de la Vieille Juiverie (old Jewry street) that lay between the present rue St.-Séverin and rue Monsieur-le-Prince. Bear in mind that Paris looked very different back then. Though many of these old Latin Quarter streets have indeed been around in some form since the sixth century, they were surrounded by fields and open spaces rather than just other streets. Imagine the area without the boulevard St.-Germain and the boulevard St.-Michel, two wide streets that were constructed in the nineteenth century. Narrow lanes and streets similar to the tangle you see off those two boulevards today are more typical of what the area looked like back then. At the corner of the boulevard St. Michel and the rue Monsieur-le-Prince there was a Jewish cemetery, and nearby a synagogue. It is believed that another Jewish cemetery was located on the tiny rue Pierre-Sarrazin just off the boulevard St.-Michel.

In the heart of Paris, on the Ile de la Cité, there was a Jewish quarter in the twelfth century. The present rue de la Cité was then called the rue des Juifs, and it, the quai de la Corse, and the rue de Lutèce delineated the quarter. Today's Marché aux Fleurs (flower market) on place Louis Lépine was where the synagogue stood.

But while Paris has been a place of Jewish greatness, prosperity, and learning, it has also seen a lot of Jewish tears. For centuries, the Jewish community lived within France only at the sufferance of the king. Expulsions were common, and it was not until Napoleon came to power that Jews finally had some measure of civil and religious freedom.

Take the story of Jonathan, a Jewish moneylender in thirteenth-century Paris. In 1290, Jonathan made a small loan to a neighbor. The woman had difficulty paying the debt, so she gave him her clothing as collateral. But once she repaid the loan, she spread nasty rumors about Jonathan. She told people that he refused to return her clothing unless she gave him the Easter communion Host from the Church of St.-Merri (in the 4th arrondissement). According to her story, she gave it to him and he hacked it with a knife until it bled. Then he threw it into a vat of boiling water, which in turn became red. At that moment, according to the woman's tale, the Host flew up out of the vat and hovered over her. She ran from Jonathan's house screaming that the house was possessed and told this story to the entire neighborhood. As a result, Jonathan was burned at the stake and his house and property were seized and destroyed. Soon after, a chapel was built on the site—now the Protestant church of Les Billettes at 22–24, rue des Archives (in the 4th arrondissement). Jonathan and his family were not the only ones to suffer in this incident: The whole Jewish community was accused along with him, and it could very well have contributed to the expulsion in 1306. This story is well illustrated in drawings and manuscripts of the time, including in the fourteenth-century Florentine manuscript the Chronicle of Giovanni Villani.[6]

The blood libel, which began against the Jews of Blois in 1171, eventually spread to Paris. Though King Louis VII was able to prevent slaughter and persecution just then, he was not able to prevent the legacy of the libel from becoming part of the public mind-set.

During the periods between expulsions, some Jews resided in Paris, and the Parisian rabbinate was highly regarded in the Jewish world. Paris was home to a number of noted Jewish scholars, among them Rabbi Shlomo ben Meir (known as the Rashbam), Rabbi Jacob ben Meir Tam, Mattathias Gaon, Chaim ben Hananel ha Kohen, Elijah ben Judah, and Jacob ben Simeon.

Following the expulsion of 1182, the Jews returned to France in 1198 and settled in and around the rue des Juifs (the present rue Ferdinand-Duval) in what is now the 4th arrondissement. Though Jews have not inhabited this area continuously since that time, it is today a heavily Jewish area and has been since 1900. A late-twelfth-century Jewish community also could be found on what are now the rue de Moussy, rue du Renard, rue St.-Merri, and rue de la Tacherie, and on the Petit Pont, or small bridge. (In those days, Paris's bridges were just like streets and were covered with houses.) Indeed, at the time, Jews lived on many other streets, and there were place-names such as Moulin aux Juifs (Jews' windmill), Ile aux Juifs (Jews' Island), and Cour de la Juiverie (Jewery court).

The Trial of the Talmud

In 1240 an infamous trial of the Talmud took place in Paris in which the Talmud was convicted and then executed in the Place de Grève (now the Place de l'Hôtel-de-Ville) by the burning of some twenty-four cartloads of Jewish books two years later.

An actual trial with a prosecutor (Church officials), defendant (the Talmud), and defendants' counsel (two rabbis), it took the form of a religious debate, or disputation, wherein those defending the Talmud were forced to defend not only its vast texts, but Judaism as a faith.

Such religious disputations were not uncommon and took place throughout France and the rest of Europe. In every case the format was the same: Jews were called upon to publicly defend their faith and their holy texts. But this particular trial was infamous for other reasons, too: A Jew, Nicholas Donin, instigated it. Donin was a student of the noted scholar Rabbi Jehiel ben Joseph (head of the Paris yeshiva and one of the two rabbis who was permitted to speak in defense of the Talmud during the trial), but he was banished from the Jewish community because of his views on the Oral Law. (A somewhat difficult concept, the Oral Law is an authoritative interpretation of the Torah and is looked upon as coexisting with the written Torah. Together they make up two aspects of the same entity for traditional Jews.) He converted to Christianity, joined the Franciscan order, and set about to exact revenge on the community that ousted him by compiling some thirty-five accusations against the Talmud. So traumatic was this trial and its outcome that it was included in the roster of disasters that have befallen the Jewish people that are recalled each year on the fast day of Tisha B'Av (the fast of the ninth day of the Hebrew month of

Av). Donin, not incidentally, was also instrumental in spread-
ing blood libel accusations around the same period.

A number of historical documents from the late twelfth century, including tax registers, paint a portrait of the economic life of
Parisian Jewry—some one hundred families. Most had come from
the provinces, and there were also a handful of refugees from
among the Jews expelled from England despite the prohibition
against it. Whereas most of the Jews were moneylenders and in
such middleman businesses as brokerage, there were more than a
few physicians in the bunch. Though their income was far above
average, the heavy taxes imposed on them by the Crown threw
most into poverty. The relative handful of Jews returning to Paris
in 1315 following the expulsion of 1306 were subject to the huge
fine imposed on all the Jews of France in 1321. But by then, Paris as
any sort of a Jewish center had declined to the point where the
Paris yeshiva could no longer claim any notable rabbis.

There was no organized Jewish community in Paris during the
fifteenth and sixteenth centuries (though a handful of Jews probably did live very discreetly in the capital), and Jews did not petition
for permission to conduct business in Paris until the early eighteenth century, when the Jews of Metz began to do so. Business
permits were not uncommon and many were prolonged to the
point where a few Jews claimed Paris as a residence. Most lived in
the relatively luxurious neighborhoods of St. Germain and St.
André.

In addition, Jews from Bordeaux who had originally come as
refugees from Spain and Portugal began to arrive along with Jews
from Avignon. Between 1721 and 1772 a special custodian of
Paris's Jews was appointed by the Crown in order to more effec-
tively extort money in the form of unusual taxes and fines and
supervise the routine confiscation of Jewish goods.

There are some engaging chronicles of Jewish travelers to Paris
in the second half of the eighteenth century. One is the diary of
Haim Joseph David Azulai (known as HIDA; 1724–1806), a Kab-

balist and bibliographer born in Jerusalem. Azulai made four trips to Europe to collect funds for the rabbinical seminary in Hebron. His diary, called *Maagal Tov* (Good Path), notes that he arrived in Paris on the twenty-second of Kislev 5538 (December 22, 1777).

> The Jews enjoy tranquility; there are many Germans, many Portuguese from Bordeaux and Bayonne, and many who hail from Avignon. People pray together every Sabbath, but there is no fixed community, birds of passage for the most part resorting hither for trading purposes. The synagogues are without privilege and exist only by a miracle.[7]

Paris was also home to Jews from Alsace-Lorraine who lived primarily in the poor neighborhoods of St. Martin and St. Denis. Most subsisted on what they earned from peddling used clothes and rags. Others with higher incomes engaged in moneylending, brokerage, and the jewelry trade. In addition there were a few artisans—painters, engravers, and embroiderers.

Beginning in 1721, there were a handful of inns that prepared kosher food. They also served as synagogues because Jews were allowed to pray only in private houses. Azulai's diary refers to them and notes that he is able to find a break from his diet of hard-boiled eggs prepared by his manservant.

Around 1736, one of those innkeepers in the outlying area of La Villette (now in the 19th arrondissement) gave part of his land to the community as a cemetery, and in 1780 the Bordeaux Jews bought the adjacent plot. The Ashkenazim bought a plot of land in Montrouge for the same purpose. And then in 1788, the first official synagogue was dedicated on the rue de Brisemiche in the 4th arrondissement.

Just prior to the French Revolution, when the leaders of the Jewish community presented their demands for full citizenship to the legislature, Paris was home to about five hundred Jews. Emancipation and freedom of movement saw the influx of Jews to Paris, and by 1809 the population had grown to twenty-nine hundred.

Most lived in the present 3rd and 4th arrondissements, as many do today. In 1819, when construction on the first Great Synagogue was begun on the rue Notre Dame de Nazareth (in the 9th arrondissement), the population was about sixty-five hundred. The synagogue was not large enough for very long, and the new (and present) Great Synagogue on the rue de la Victoire (in the 9th arrondissement) was completed in 1877 along with another on the rue des Tournelles (in the 4th arrondissement).

Paris's Jewish community in the mid- and late nineteenth century was thriving. The rabbinical seminary had been moved to Paris from Metz, and primary schools had been established, along with charitable organizations and Jewish newspapers. Some thirty thousand Jews lived in Paris and they made up about 40 percent of the entire Jewish population of France. Of that thirty thousand, most had come originally from the cities and towns of Alsace-Lorraine and from Germany, but there were a few hundred from Poland. Most Jews were middle class and were employed as peddlers, merchants, and secondhand goods dealers, along with a growing number of tailors, milliners, and shoemakers. In addition, the number of Jewish lawyers, doctors, and university professors was increasing.

The defeat of France in the Franco-Prussian War in 1871 and the loss of Alsace and part of Lorraine cut the Jewish population of France to about sixty thousand, but refugees from Poland, Russia, Austria, and Romania added to that figure and shortly the Jewish majority, those originally from Alsace and Lorraine, became the minority. Between the two world wars following the fall of the Ottoman Empire, immigration to France, and to Paris in particular, came from North Africa, Turkey, and the Balkans. On the eve of World War II there were about 150,000 Jews in Paris—more than half the Jewish population of France. Jews lived all over Paris, but most of the Jewish neighborhoods were in the northern and eastern parts of the city, as they are today.

Parisian Jewry suffered terribly during the Nazi occupation, when thousands of Jews were rounded up, processed at the now demolished Vélodrome d'Hiver (winter bicycle stadium), moved to the transit camp at Drancy, and shipped to their deaths in Auschwitz and other camps. At war's end, the Jewish community and its institutions were in shambles. Rebuilding did not come easily, but it did come.

Paris at the dawn of the new millennium is home to 2.5 million people; counting the surrounding suburbs, which have become as much a part of Paris as Paris proper, the total is some 10.5 million. The Jewish community numbers about 375,000 and it represents about 8 percent of the Paris total. Although some neighborhoods are distinctly Jewish, Jews can be found in every part of the city and the suburbs. Areas with the largest organized communities are in the 4th, 9th, 11th, 13th, 19th, and 20th arrondissements. Today, most Jews no longer practice such traditional Jewish occupations as small merchants and craftsmen; they can be found in every sector of French life and economy and they are an integral part of Paris's vibrant intellectual community.

4th Arrondissement

MÉTRO: CITÉ

Begin your walk at Ile de la Cité in front of Notre Dame

Nearby (non-Jewish) sights: Notre Dame, the Palais de Justice, Sainte Chapelle, the Horloge quarter, Ile St. Louis

THIS IS THE HEART of Paris, and the heart of France. The square in front of Notre Dame de Paris, known as the Parvis, is the place from which all distances in France are measured. Though Paris contains countless vestiges of the Jewish past, there is a lack of specifically Jewish architectural monuments as a result of the long-enforced absences of the Jewish community. Nonetheless, evidence of the Jewish presence is here even on some churches.

The eastern part of the Ile de la Cité has for many centuries had spiritual significance for Parisians. Back in the Middle Ages one could count over twenty churches in the area and even one synagogue. But King Philippe-Auguste converted the synagogue into a church when he confiscated all Jewish property and possessions in order to raise money to construct the central market at Les Halles.

In the twelfth century, this Jewish quarter was bounded by the present rue de la Cité (known then as the rue des Juifs), the quai de la Corse, and the rue de Lutèce. The synagogue was on the site of today's Marché aux Fleurs (flower market) on Place Louis Lépine. The rue de la Cité also was Roman Lutetia's main road. Look south toward the Left Bank. The rue de la Cité becomes the rue du Petit Pont and then the rue St. Jacques on the other side of the Petit Pont. The rue St. Jacques (St. James) was the main road to the south and was so named because it eventually led to Spain and Santiago de Compostella, resting place of the bones of St. James (Santiago), a major medieval pilgrimage destination. Pilgrims brought back local scallop shells as proof that they had been there. (The dish Coquilles [scallops] St. Jacques gets its name from that, but we'll leave that to another book; shellfish are hardly appropriate for this one.)

When the king expelled the Jews from France in 1182, it marked the end of the Jewish presence on the Ile de la Cité. Sixteen years later, in 1198, the same Philippe-Auguste invited the Jews back so he could take more money from them for other royal projects. This time, they settled not on the Ile de la Cité, but in other parts of the city. Some settled on the Left Bank, where there had been a history of Jewish settlement (see the 5th arrondissement section), but most went to the Right Bank, where Paris was developing. There they settled on rue Saint-Bon just south of the present Church of Saint-Merri. From there they eventually spread out to the neighborhood around the rue des Rosiers.

SIGHTS

Notre Dame de Paris

Notre Dame de Paris is one of the most famous sights in all of Paris and certainly one of the most spectacular. Its imposing stone façade, towers, and flying buttresses have been painted and photographed from every conceivable angle. It is also an enduring symbol of French Catholicism and the seat of the Paris archbishopric. So it is surprising that this standard-bearer of the Roman Catholic Church in France also holds quite a bit of interest for Jews.

In front of the cathedral you can easily see the figures on the façade. On either side of the central portal, in tall niches, are two female figures known as Ecclesia and Synagoga. On the left as you face the portal is Ecclesia—a beautiful woman wearing a crown. She represents the Roman Catholic Church. On the right side of the portal is Synagoga—a woman blinded by a serpent around her eyes, with her head bowed, and her staff shattered. She represents Judaism. From Synagoga's hand slip the tablets of the Ten Commandments. These two figures are common in church architecture all over Europe (particularly in France and Germany) and represent the age-old religious conflict between Christianity and Judaism.

Another item of interest for Jews is the present archbishop of Paris himself—Jean-Marie Lustiger, born Aron Lustiger, a Jew. Natives of Poland, Lustiger's parents left Poland for Paris, where Aron was born in 1926. Both his parents were deported during the Nazi occupation and killed in Auschwitz.

Statue of Synagoga, Notre Dame de Paris

Like many French Jewish children, Aron was placed with a Christian family for safety during the German occupation in World War II. In 1940 he was baptized a Catholic and changed his name to Jean-Marie. Educated at La Sorbonne (the University of Paris) and Paris's Institut Catholique, he was ordained a priest in 1954. He became archbishop of Paris in 1981 and was created a cardinal by Pope John Paul II in 1983.

Cardinal Lustiger's conversion to Christianity mirrors that of other Jewish children who, because their parents believed their physical safety lay in the hands of Christians, gave up or were forced to give up their birthright at the very time when the survival of the Jewish people was threatened. It continues to be a very sore point in relations between Judaism and the Catholic Church.

Memorial to the Deported

Behind Notre Dame there is a garden, Square Jean XXIII, named for Pope John XXIII (1958–63). The garden continues across the quai de l'Archevêché, but its name changes to Square de l'Ile de France. There is a small gate on the right side of the square (with your back to the cathedral) that leads to the small memorial. Washed by the lapping waters of the Seine, it holds the tomb of the unknown deportee. Inside are the names of the German death camps where 200,000 French men, women, and children, Jews and Christians, were put to death. It is a moving memorial—simple yet poignant. As you leave, the words above the door speak volumes: PARDONNE MAIS N'OUBLIE PAS: "Forgive, but do not forget!"

The next part of this tour is in another section of the 4th arrondissement. You can take the Métro to the St. Paul stop or you can walk, but it's a hike. Begin at the corner of rue de Rivoli and rue Pavée (Métro: St. Paul).

The Pletzl

A good time to come here is in the late morning or early afternoon on Friday, when residents are busy preparing for the Sabbath and the streets are busy and lively. But keep it in mind for Sunday, too, when many Paris restaurants are closed. You can always find a meal or a snack here, as well as prepared food to take back to your hotel or have as a picnic in one of Paris's ubiquitous parks and squares. But be aware that the narrow rue des Rosiers is so crowded on Sunday that it's difficult to walk.

This neighborhood is known, affectionately, as the Pletzl—Yiddish for *little place*. It, along with the larger area surrounding it, is known as the Marais (the swamp). Centuries ago, Paris's ground level was much closer to the level of the river and this section of town was swampland. This part of Paris's 4th arrondissement is a tangle of streets centered on the rue des Rosiers, and it is here where you will find many Jewish shops and restaurants. In more modern times, Ashkenazic (eastern European) Jews and Sephardic Jews from North Africa have lived around here since the early twentieth century. But this was a Jewish neighborhood in the Middle Ages, too. In the thirteenth century it was known as La Juiverie (the Jewry), and in it was a thriving and fairly self-sufficient community complete with synagogues, cemeteries, and food manufacturers. Some of the street names from that early period survive, as we shall see later in the walk.

In the thirteenth and fourteenth centuries, the Jews of this area led a precarious existence punctuated by successive expulsions and returns according to the whims or economic calculations of monarchs. But that ended in 1394 with their final (for that period) expulsion from France. Of course, some Jews were able to take advantage of loopholes in the ban, so there was never a time when there were no Jews in Paris at all. This is why Louis XIII had to reiterate the ban in 1615. Such surreptitious residence in the capital ended only with the emancipation of the Jews on September 27, 1791.

Until the late seventeenth century, this district was full of grand mansions and beautiful vistas—the center of residential life for Paris's movers and shakers. But in the 1680s the French court moved from the Louvre (then a royal palace) to Versailles, and the rich and powerful moved away from the Marais in order to be closer to court. As is the case with many fashionable neighborhoods throughout history and throughout the world, the exodus of the moneyed classes signaled the decline of the Marais as a desirable spot to live.

When the nineteenth century brought industrialization to western European cities, the mansions of the Marais were carved up into small apartments and workshops. It wasn't long before crowded conditions became even more so as hovels cropped up in courtyards, in the fronts of houses, and even on rooftops. The once

Synagogue on rue Pavée in the Pletzl

glitzy Marais had become a fetid slum with precious little sunlight. Many of the residents were Jews, the descendants of those who had been expelled in the twelfth century by Philippe-Auguste.

But look around you. Urban history has interesting twists and turns. The Marais is now one of Paris's hottest and trendiest quarters and real estate prices here are very high as successful artists, media types, and celebrities vie for a piece of this historic area. Unlike many old Paris neighborhoods, the Marais remains relatively free of the sort of development that has changed them from quaint to garish. Here, most renovation takes place on the inside, with cosmetic work on the exteriors.

During World War II, Jews were deported from this and other Parisian neighborhoods. Some of those who were lucky enough to survive returned after the liberation and filed legal actions for the return of their homes and shops that had been appropriated by the occupying Germans and then the French. Now, once again, it is a vibrant center of Parisian Jewish life. As you walk look for plaques on some buildings commemorating individuals and families who were deported and did not return. It took many years for the relatives of those people to get the city of Paris to agree to these memorials.

Turn on to rue Pavée. At number 10 is Agudath Hakehilot (01-48-87-49-03), home to an Orthodox Ashkenazic congregation. Built in 1914 and designed by Hector Guimard—the Art Nouveau architect and decorator famous for the green vegetal archways he made for the Paris Métro stations—this is the largest synagogue in the Pletzl. Guimard's wife, an American, was Jewish and with the rise of Nazism they left France for the United States. On Yom Kippur, 1940, it was dynamited by the Germans, but it has since been restored and is now a national monument in addition to playing a key role in the community. Note, too, that during the French Revolution the prison of La Force, used to detain political prisoners, stood nearby at the site of the present 14–22, rue Mahler.

Continue along the rue Pavée to the rue des Rosiers, and turn left. Along this narrow, ancient street you will find kosher and Jewish-style restaurants cheek by jowl with Jewish bookshops, small synagogues, prayer rooms, and kosher boulangeries and charcuteries. At the part of the street closest to the rue Pavée you will also see trendy shops, a sign of the increasingly gentrified nature of the neighborhood.

Off the rue des Rosiers, on your left, is the rue Ferdinand Duval, which was the rue des Juifs until 1900. In the rear of the courtyard of number 20 (the door may be locked) is a sixteenth-century hôtel particulier (a large private house) known as the Hôtel des Juifs. Now owned by an artist, it is a remnant of a Jewish community of the eighteenth century composed of Jews from Alsace, Lorraine, and Germany.

Retrace your steps back to the rue des Rosiers, turn left, and continue to the rue des Ecouffes (street of kites—a bird of prey and an archaic and derisive term for pawnbroker), which will be on your left. There are a number of Orthodox synagogues along this short street that begins down at the rue de Rivoli and ends at the rue des Rosiers. You will also notice the posters of the late Lubavitcher Rebbe, Menachem Mendel Schneerson. Many Lubavitcher Hasidim live in this neighborhood, and their worldwide followers are a strong presence here and elsewhere in Paris.

At the corner of rue des Ecouffes and rue des Rosiers is a good kosher charcuterie, B. Finkelstajn's. The somewhat famous Jo Goldenberg's (not kosher) is up the street. Unfortunately, this decades-old eatery lives on its fame despite the quality of its food. It's a photo-op spot for politicians, and a destination for hordes of tourists in a futile search for a good Jewish meal.

Go back to the rue des Rosiers, turn left, and walk to rue des Hospitalières-St.-Gervais. Turn right. A short distance up the street on your right (number 6) is a Jewish boys' school. The plaque on the wall commemorates the students and teachers of this school who were sent to the internment camp at Drancy and then to Auschwitz, where they were murdered. One hundred sixty-five boys were deported from here, despite the headmaster's efforts to save as many as he could.

A short distance away is the rue des Archives and the church of Les Billettes, site of the house of the ill-fated Jonathan (see the beginning of this chapter for more on this story).

You can now visit the Memorial to the Unknown Jewish Martyr at the Centre de Documentation Juive Contemporaine (Jewish Contemporary Documentation Center) a short walk away or you can continue on to the synagogues near the place des Vosges.

If you turn right at the next corner, the rue des Francs Bourgeois, you can take a leisurely stroll along that street, past the rue de Turenne, until you get to the enchanting place des Vosges. The walk from rue des Francs Bourgeois will take you to the northern part of the place. On the eastern side of the square, at 14, place des Vosges, is the lovely synagogue Temple des Vosges (01-48-87-79-45). You will know it only from the address. As is the case with many synagogues in Paris, there is nothing on the outside to indicate what's behind the building's façade. Around the corner at 21 bis, rue des Tournelles, directly in back of the Temple des Vosges, is another synagogue (01-42-74-32-65 or 01-42-74-32-80), built in 1876 and known for the wrought-iron interior by Gustave Eiffel. The Temple des Vosges is Ashkenazic and the other is Sephardic.

To visit the Memorial of the Unknown Jewish Martyr and Documentation Center (01-42-77-44-72) from the rue des Hospitalières-St.-Gervais, retrace your steps along the rue des Rosiers to the rue des Ecouffes and turn right. Continue to the rue de Rivoli, cross it, and you will find yourself on the rue Tiron. Continue a very short distance to the rue François-Miron and turn right. Another short distance will bring you to the rue Geoffroy-l'Asnier. Turn left. The memorial is number 17.

This is one of the most moving Jewish sites in Paris. It stands as a memorial to the nearly six million Jews who were murdered by the Germans and their accomplices. Begun in Grenoble during World War II (see chapter 10) as a means of documenting German atrocities, the museum has been expanded over the years since it was built in 1956 and contains displays of documents and photographs of Nazi camps. The building also houses a library and archives and is a valuable research institution.

The Museum of Jewish Art and History

Not far away, at 71, rue du Temple (in the 3rd arrondissement; Métro: Hôtel-de-Ville), is the new Musée d'Art et d'Histoire du Judaïsme. Tel: 01-53-01-86-53. Hours: Monday–Friday, 11 A.M. to 6 P.M. Closed Saturdays and Jewish holidays. Opened with much publicity in December 1998, the museum is dedicated to the celebration of Jewish life in the extensive picture exhibits and collection of ritual objects. There is also a huge model of Solomon's Temple in Jerusalem. The museum's library provides rich resources for scholars. Future planned exhibits (as of this writing) include the wandering Jew in Western society, art, and popular culture. To get to the museum from the Memorial of the

Unknown Jewish Martyr, walk back to the rue de Rivoli and take the Métro from the St. Paul station to the Hôtel-de-Ville station. Or, walk back to the rue de Rivoli and turn left onto it. When you get to the rue du Temple, make a right. But just before you turn onto the rue du Temple, you may want to make a detour to the left, across the rue de Rivoli, to the square in front of the Hôtel-de-Ville (city hall). That was the former Place de Grève, where the trial of the Talmud was held in 1240.

To get to the museum from the center of the Marais, follow either the rue Pavée or the rue des Hospitalières-St.-Gervais to the rue des Francs Bourgeois and turn left. Continue along the rue des Francs Bourgeois as it becomes the rue Rambuteau on the other side of the rue des Archives. When you get to the corner of the rue Rambuteau and the rue du Temple, turn right. The museum is a block away. Don't make the mistake of turning onto the rue Vieille-du-Temple.

3RD AND 4TH ARRONDISSEMENT RESOURCES

Synagogues: 3rd Arrondissement

All have daily morning and evening minyan; Shabbat and festival minyan.

Centre Israel Jeffrokyn. 70, rue de Turbigo.
Tel: 01-44-61-29-15.

Synagogue. 15, rue Notre Dame de Nazareth.
Tel: 01-42-78-00-30.

Synagogues: 4th Arrondissement

All have daily morning and evening minyan; Shabbat and festival minyan.

Adath Yechouroun. 25, rue des Rosiers.
Tel: 01-44-59-82-36 (Polish).

Temple des Vosges. 14, place des Vosges.
Tel: 01-48-87-79-45.

Synagogue. 21 bis, rue des Tournelles.
Tel: 01-42-74-32-65 or 01-42-74-32-80.

Synagogue Aqudath Hakehilos. 10, rue Pavée.
Tel: 01-48-87-21-54.

Mikvah: 3rd Arrondissement

176, rue du Temple. Tel: 01-42-71-89-28.

Kosher Food

All food shops and restaurants listed here are under the supervision of the Beth Din of Paris and/or Rabbi M. Rottenberg, chief rabbi of the Paris Orthodox Chief Rabbinate. This is only a partial listing. All kosher food shops and restaurants must display their supervision in the window. Except where otherwise indicated, all restaurants serve North African and Israeli food.

Kosher Restaurants: 3rd Arrondissement

Café du Musée d'Art et d'Histoire du Judaïsme. 1, rue du Temple. Tel: 01-53-01-86-53.

Café Ninette. 24, rue Notre Dame de Nazareth.
Tel: 01-42-72-08-56.

Meat. Eat in or take out.

Les Tables de la Loi. 15, rue St.-Gilles.
Tel: 01-48-04-38-02.

Meat, French cuisine. Eat in or take out.

Ma Toque. 76, rue Charlot. Tel: 01-48-04-76-76.

 Dairy, sandwiches. Eat in or take out.

Beverly Café. 73, rue de Turbigo. Tel: 01-42-72-93-33.

 Meat. Eat in or take out. Open only for lunch.

Kosher Restaurants: 4th Arrondissement

Café des Psaumes. 14, rue des Rosiers.
Tel: 01-48-04-74-77.

 Meat. Eat in or take out.

Contini. 42, rue des Rosiers. Tel: 01-48-04-78-32.

 Meat, sandwiches.

Hamman Café. 4, rue des Rosiers.
Tel: 01-42-78-04-46 or 01-48-87-25-19.

 Dairy.

JB. 19, rue Ferdinand Duval. Tel: 01-42-71-72-82.

 Meat.

Korcarz. 29, rue des Rosiers. Tel: 01-42-77-39-47.

 Fish.

Koscher Pizza. 1, rue des Rosiers. Tel: 01-48-87-17-83.

 Dairy.

La Petite Famille. 32, rue des Rosiers.
Tel: 01-42-77-00-50.

 Meat.

La Pita. 26, rue des Rosiers. Tel: 01-42-77-93-13.

 Meat.

Mezel. 1, rue Ferdinand Duval. Tel: 01-42-78-25-01.

Meat.

Micky's Deli. 23 bis, rue des Rosiers.
Tel: 01-48-04-79-31 or 01-48-87-14-07.

Meat.

O'Bar. 14, rue Pavée. Tel: 01-48-04-39-15.

Dairy, Jewish traditional.

Tutti Frutti. 38, rue des Rosiers. Tel: 01-42-76-04-75.

Dairy, fish, sandwiches.

Yahalom. 22, rue des Rosiers.
Tel: 01-42-77-12-35 or 01-42-77-21-00.

Meat.

Kosher Takeout: 4th Arrondissement

Panzer Dimitri. 26, rue des Rosiers.
Tel: 01-40-27-82-75 or 01-42-72-91-06.

Sfez. 8, rue St.-Antoine. Tel: 01-42-71-51-95.

Bookstores: 4th Arrondissement

Bazar Suzanne. 14, rue Ferdinand Duval.
Tel: 01-48-87-34-84 or 01-60-58-34-84.

Bibliophane. 26, rue des Rosiers. Tel: 01-48-87-82-20.

Chir Hadach. 1, rue des Hospitalières-St.-Gervais.
Tel: 01-42-72-38-00.

Diasporama. 20, rue des Rosiers. Tel: 01-42-78-30-50.

Librairie du Marais. 7, rue des Rosiers.
Tel: 01-48-87-99-97.

Librairie du Progrès. 23, rue des Ecouffes.
Tel: 01-42-72-94-44.

Librairie Hébraica Judaica. 12, rue des Hospitalières-St.-
Gervais. Tel: 01-48-87-32-20.

Librairie Tal. 19, rue Ferdinand Duval.
Tel: 01-42-78-64-46.

5th and 6th Arrondissements

MÉTRO: ST. MICHEL

The 5th arrondissement, generally referred to as the Latin Quarter, is one of Paris's oldest areas of habitation. Many of the winding streets you see in this neighborhood, particularly those closest to the Seine, are hundreds of years old. So it is no surprise that the earliest Jewish inhabitants of Paris made their homes here along with the other residents.

Perhaps the earliest known synagogue was in the sixth century C.E. It stood in the vicinity of the present Church of St.-Julien-le-Pauvre (on the rue St.-Julien-le-Pauvre), one of the oldest churches in Paris, just across the river from Notre Dame. Nothing is really known about that community except that it existed. Nothing remains of it.

A few hundred years later, in the tenth and eleventh centuries, a community of Jews lived in the same neighborhood on the present rue de la Harpe between the rue de la Huchette and the rue St.-Séverin. The story goes that rue de la Harpe (harp players street) was named for King David, whose image was on a local street sign in the thirteenth century. The synagogue was on the corner of what is now the boulevard St.-Michel and rue Monsieur-le-Prince, and the community lived between what is now the rue Monsieur-le-

Prince and rue St.-Séverin on rue de la Vieille Juiverie (old Jewry street). The cemetery was nearby on the present rue Pierre-Sarrazin. Confused? Keep in mind that Paris looked very different back then. Though many of these old streets have indeed been around for that long, fields and open spaces surrounded them. To give you a little bit of an idea, try to imagine this area without the boulevard St.-Michel and the boulevard St.-Germain. When those two wide streets were constructed in the nineteenth century, countless small streets and alleys were bulldozed to make way for them.

SIGHTS

Museum

Musée National du Moyen Age. 6, place Paul Painlevé. Tel: 01-43-25-62-00. Hours: 9:15 A.M. to 5:45 P.M. Closed Tuesdays. Tours in English on Wednesdays at 12:30.

Housed in the Hôtel de Cluny, and built on the site of first-century Roman baths, this was once a medieval monastery. It has a wonderful collection of medieval illuminated manuscripts, tapestries, and other items of interest to the medievalist. One of its holdings is a gilded enamel copper disk, circa 1170. It's a crucifix with Ecclesia and Synagoga. The inscription around the disk reads *hec parit, hec credit, obit hic, fugit hec, his obedit* (Mary gives birth, Ecclesia believes, Christ dies, Synagoga flees, John obeys).[8]

Rabbinical Seminary

Séminaire Israélite de France. 9, rue Vauquelin.
Tel: 01-47-07-21-22.

The Consistoire's rabbinical seminary.

5TH AND 6TH ARRONDISSEMENT RESOURCES

Synagogues: 5th Arrondissement

Centre Rachi. 30, boulevard de Port-Royal.
Tel: 01-43-31-98-20.

> Daily morning minyan; Shabbat and festival minyan.

Seminaire Israélite de France. 9, rue Vauquelin.
Tel: 01-47-07-21-22.

Synagogue: 6th Arrondissement

Centre Edmond Fleg. 8 bis, rue de l'Eperon.
Tel: 01-46-33-43-31.

> This is Paris's student center.

Mikvah: 5th Arrondissement

50, rue Lacépède. Tel: 01-45-35-26-90.

Kosher Restaurants (Beth Din supervision): 5th Arrondissement

Giorgio. 50, rue Broca. Tel: 01-43-36-87-03.

> Dairy, snacks, sandwiches.

Cafétéria de l'Espace Rachi. 39, rue Broca.
Tel: 01-42-17-11-51.

> Meat, snacks.

Kosher Restaurant: 6th Arrondissement

Centre Edmond Fleg. 8 bis, rue de l'Eperon.
Tel: 01-46-33-43-31.

Meat. Takeout. This is Paris's student center.

7th Arrondissement

MÉTRO: ECOLE MILITAIRE

Nearby sights: Ecole Militaire, Napoleon's Tomb, the
Eiffel Tower

*T*HE COURTYARD of the Ecole Militaire (military academy) was the scene of the culmination of one of the most
notorious incidents in modern French history. It was here on January 5, 1895, that Captain Alfred Dreyfus was publicly stripped of
his rank and uniform and dishonored following a sham trial (see
chapter 1). Over the shouts of "mort aux juifs" (death to the Jews)
by the angry crowds and anti-Jewish jeers by his fellow officers,
Dreyfus continued to proclaim his innocence. Though he was
eventually cleared, reinstated in the army, and promoted, his rein-
statement ceremony didn't get nearly as much press as the one at
which he was dishonored—and it didn't take place in the main
courtyard. It is ironic that among the officers who subsequently
trained at the Ecole Militaire were Israel's Moshe Dayan and
Chaim Bar Lev.

7TH ARRONDISSEMENT RESOURCES

Kosher Food

La Grande Epicerie de Paris, in the Bon Marché department store. 38, rue de Sèvres. Tel: 01-44-39-81-00. Métro: Sèvres-Babylone. Hours: 8:30 A.M. to 9:30 P.M. Closed Sunday.

This wonderful and huge food shop, which sells all manner of fresh, packaged, and prepared foods, has a small kosher section. Most of the stuff is Israeli and you can get canned goods, wine, crackers, chocolate, and other munchies. It's located toward the front of the store as you walk in, near the cash registers. Look for the sign that says *casher* (Kosher).

9th Arrondissement

MÉTRO: CADET

Walk southwest on rue Cadet to the intersection of the rue du Faubourg-Montmartre, the rue Cadet, and the rue Richer. If the street name changes to rue de Rochechouart, you've gone in the wrong direction.

Nearby sights: Montmartre, Sacré-Coeur, Musée Grévin, Passage Jouffroy, Opéra Garnier, Grands Boulevards, Folies-Bergère

JUST BELOW what was once the village of Montmartre, with its steep hills, winding streets, working vineyard, and one of Paris's only remaining windmills, is an area known as lower Montmartre. It is here that you will find another Jewish quarter in and around the intersection of the rue du Faubourg-Montmartre, the rue Cadet, and the rue Richer. Though this neighborhood doesn't have the history or the quaint character of the Marais, it is no less Jewish. And don't be put off by what can look like shabby building façades. They often are just that: façades. Though this is not generally a ritzy area, inside the heavy outer doors of some buildings you will find quaint courtyards leading to some lovely apartments, particularly on the streets just off the main commercial ones. (This is true all over Paris.)

This area developed as a Jewish neighborhood in the middle of the nineteenth century when Jews from eastern Europe began to arrive. Today these streets are lined with Jewish shops and restaurants and there are easily a dozen synagogues on nearby streets. Though most of the restaurants serve Israeli or North African food, there is the occasional French and even kosher Chinese and kosher Tex-Mex. Nearby are a number of notable synagogues and the offices of the Consistoire Central.

SIGHTS

Rue Buffault Synagogue

At the intersection of the rue du Faubourg-Montmartre, the rue Cadet, and the rue Richer, with the rue Richer on your right and the rue de Provence across the street on your left, walk straight to the rue Buffault, which will be on your right. At number 28 is a synagogue built in 1877. The design of the façade is typical of synagogues built throughout France at the time: arched doorways crowned by a rose window. If you go inside you will see the bimah (the raised area from which services are conducted and from which the Torah is read) in the center of the room. This is also typical of French synagogues, in contrast with the ones you may be familiar with in the United States that have the bimah in front. Wooden pews and chandeliers also characterize the interior.

Kosher butcher, rue Richer, Paris, 9th arrondissement

Rue de la Victoire Synagogue

Retrace your steps back along the rue Buffault to the rue du Faubourg-Montmartre, turn right, and walk to where the rue Drouot crops out on the left side of the street. Cross the rue Lafayette and you will see the rue de la Victoire on your left. Turn left and walk to number 44, the Synagogue de la Victoire, also known as the Rothschild synagogue. It is on the site of a grand eighteenth-century mansion that was purchased by the Jewish community and torn down.

Just around the corner from the offices of the Consistoire Central at 17, rue St.-Georges, the synagogue was originally supposed to open onto the rue de Châteaudun, but Empress Eugénie (the wife of Napoleon III) deemed it unseemly for a Jewish house of worship to be located between two nearby churches—Notre Dame de Lorette and Sainte Trinité.

Built in 1874 with a Romanesque façade, the synagogue was needed because the one on the rue Notre-Dame-de-Nazareth (in the 3rd arrondissement) was too crowded and the Jewish population was growing rapidly. The interior of the synagogue is the real showpiece. Yellow, blue, and red circular stained-glass windows allow the most magnificent light to stream into this cathedral-like sanctuary with its eighty-seven-foot ceilings. The bimah is reached by a few stairs and is flanked by seats reserved for Paris's and France's chief rabbis. A vaulted dome covers the ark.

9TH ARRONDISSEMENT RESOURCES

Synagogues

28, rue Buffault. Tel: 01-45-26-80-87.

Daily morning and evening minyan; Shabbat and festival minyan.

Synagogue de la Victoire (aka the Rothschild synagogue). 44, rue de la Victoire. Tel: 01-40-82-26-26.

Daily morning and evening minyan; Shabbat and festival minyan.

Mikvaot

6, rue Ambroise-Thomas. Tel: 01-48-24-86-94.

8, rue Lamartine. Tel: 01-45-26-87-60.

Kosher Restaurants (Beth Din supervision)

Adolphe. 14, rue Richer. Tel: 01-47-70-91-25.
Meat.

Azar & Fils. 6, rue Geoffroy-Marie. Tel: 01-47-70-08-38.
Meat.

Casa Rina. 8, rue du Faubourg-Montmartre.
Tel: 01-45-23-02-22.

Dairy, Italian.

Chez Jonathan. 24, rue du Faubourg-Montmartre.
Tel: 01-48-24-23-04.

Meat, fish.

Cine Citta Café. 58, rue Richer. Tel: 01-42-46-09-65.

Dairy, Italian.

Le Bistrot Blanc. 52, rue Blanche. Tel: 01-42-85-05-30.

Dairy, fish.

Mao Tsur. 10 bis, rue Geoffroy-Marie.
Tel: 01-48-01-65-65.

Meat, Chinese.

Yankees Café. 31, rue du Faubourg-Montmartre.
Tel: 01-42-46-52-46.

Meat, Tex-Mex.

Bookstores

Beth Hassofer. 52, rue Richer. Tel: 01-45-23-22-49.

La Foire du Livre. 37, rue Richer. Tel: 01-47-70-38-53.

Librairie Colbo. 3, rue Richer. Tel: 01-47-70-21-81 or
01-47-70-60-76.

Librairie Ohr Moshe. 26, rue de Trévise.
Tel: 01-45-23-27-21.

11th Arrondissement

*I*N THIS LOWER-WORKING-CLASS CUM ultratrendy quarter around the place de la Bastille, there is yet another Jewish enclave.

After World War I, Jews from the former Ottoman Empire (Greece, Turkey, and Bulgaria) began to arrive here in great numbers. In this neighborhood of shabby hotels that provided cramped and barely basic living conditions, the Jewish immigrants made a living very much as they had in their countries of origin—as small merchants dealing in household goods and clothing.

Eastern European Jews arrived between the two world wars and established themselves in the clothing manufacturing business, and the Jewish immigrants from North Africa who arrived here beginning in the 1960s are today's heirs to those businesses. Beginning in the mid- and late 1970s, artists began to come here to take advantage of the cheap housing. Renovation began and gentrification soon followed.

11TH ARRONDISSEMENT RESOURCES

Synagogues

All these synagogues have a daily morning and evening minyan; Shabbat and festival minyan.

Synagogue don Isaac Abravanel. 84–86, rue de la Roquette. Tel: 01-47-00-75-95.

Ozar Hatorah Shoul. 40, rue de l'Orillon. Tel: 01-43-38-73-40.

Adath Israel. 36, rue Basfroi.
Tel: 01-43-67-89-20 or 01-43-48-12-86.

Kosher Restaurants (Beth Din supervision)

Cocktail Café. 82, avenue Parmentier.
Tel: 01-43-57-19-94.

Dairy, Italian.

Esteban. 103, avenue Parmentier. Tel: 01-43-38-52-82.

Provençal, Spanish.

Le Cabourg. 102, boulevard Voltaire.
Tel: 01-47-00-71-43.

Meat; fondues bourguignonnes, foie gras.

Lotus de Nissane. 39, rue Amelot. Tel: 01-43-55-80-42
or 01-43-57-44-05.

Meat, Chinese.

Yun Pana. 115, boulevard Voltaire. Tel: 01-43-79-20-48.

Meat, Vietnamese.

14th Arrondissement

MÉTRO: EDGAR-QUINET

SIGHTS

Cemetery

Montparnasse Cemetery. 3, boulevard Edgar-Quinet. Tel: 01-44-10-86-50. Hours: Daily, 9 A.M. to 5:30 P.M. Map available near the entrance.

This quiet spot sits in stark contrast to the urban character of the rest of the neighborhood. Like Paris's other cemeteries, it's a fine place to stroll and contemplate the past . . . and the present. Among the famous graves here, Alfred Dreyfus. And because death has at least as many ironies as history itself, nearby is the grave of the wife of Marshal Philippe Pétain, a man who actually did sell out France to the Germans several decades after Dreyfus was falsely accused. Other notables (non-Jewish) here for the duration as it were are filmmaker François Truffaut, Guy de Maupassant, Samuel Beckett, Charles Baudelaire, actress Jean Seberg, Statue of Liberty sculptor Frédéric Bartholdi, and Jean-Paul Sartre and Simone de Beauvoir—together in death as they were in life.

15th Arrondissement

MÉTRO: BIR-HAKEIM

SIGHTS

Place des Martyrs Juifs du Vélodrome d'Hiver

In this upper-middle-class neighborhood of high-rise apartment buildings and plenty of parks, you won't find anything of Jewish historical interest—except for one monument near the Bir-Hakeim bridge, between the quai de Grenelle and the quai Branly. It was nearby, on the rue Nélaton, that the huge Vélodrome d'Hiver (known then and now as the Vél d'Hiv) was located. An indoor stadium used for six-day bicycle races, concerts, boxing matches, and other events, it was, from 1942 until its demolition in 1958, one of the most infamous places in all Paris.

La Grande Rafle was the name given to the main roundup of all the Jews in Paris. Early on the morning of July 16, 1942, the French police, acting under orders from the German Gestapo, wrenched over thirteen thousand Jewish men, women, and children from their beds. Most of the adults were sent directly to the camp at Drancy, while parents with children went to the Vél d'Hiv. And it didn't stop then. For the next two days the French police canvassed the city with buses, picking up Jews and taking them to the stadium.

Conditions inside the Vél d'Hiv were horrendous: it was hot, there were no toilet facilities, and there was little food and no place to sleep. For six days amidst mounting panic, the horrified prisoners endured physical indignity while the French police stood by.

The place des Martyrs Juifs du Vélodrome d'Hiver was dedicated on July 17, 1994. Each year now a ceremony commemorates the shameful incident. It was here, in 1995, that President Jacques

Chirac, who had just been elected to office, officially acknowledged France's complicity in the murder and deportation of the Jews of Europe.

18th Arrondissement

MÉTRO: CLICHY OR BLANCHE

SIGHTS

Cemetery

Montmartre Cemetery. 20, avenue Rachel. Tel: 01-43-87-64-24. Hours: Daily, 8:30 A.M. to 5:30 P.M.

Another quiet place in the still charming and relatively out-of-the-way neighborhood of Montmartre, this cemetery is the final home of Heinrich Heine (who converted to Catholicism) and composer Jacques Offenbach.

20th Arrondissement

MÉTRO: PÈRE-LACHAISE

SIGHTS

Cemetery

Père-Lachaise Cemetery. 16, rue du Repos. Tel: 01-43-70-70-33. Hours: March–October, Monday–Friday, 8 A.M. to 6 P.M., Saturday, 8:30 A.M. to 6 P.M., Sunday and holidays, 9 A.M. to 6 P.M.; November–February, Monday–Friday, 8 A.M. to 5:30 P.M., Saturday, 8:30 A.M. to 5:30 P.M., Sunday and holidays, 9 A.M. to 5:30 P.M. Last visit is fifteen minutes before closing. Free. There may be maps available at the entrance booth, but in case they're not most tabacs in the neighborhood will sell you one.

Probably the most famous cemetery in Paris, and certainly the most visited, this large burial ground on the eastern edge of the city contains many ornate tombs and graves. Apart from the historical value of a visit, it's also a nice quiet spot to stroll and contemplate the history of Paris. Buried here are such giants in French history as Abélard and Héloïse and Molière (who were all reinterred here after the cemetery was opened in 1803), Balzac, Baron Haussmann, and Edith Piaf, and such disparate foreigners as Oscar Wilde, Jim Morrison, and Gertrude Stein. Famous Jews include many from the Rothschild family, actress Sarah Bernhardt, auto manufacturer André Citroën, and artist Camille Pissarro.

Outside *Paris*

MÉTRO: BOBIGNY/PABLO PICASSO

SIGHTS

Drancy Concentration Camp Memorial

The memorial is at the Cité de la Muette.

The outdoor monument was dedicated in 1976. There is also a boxcar that was used to transport Jews from the transit camp at Drancy to Auschwitz. There is an exhibit in the boxcar showing conditions at Drancy at the time Jews were interned there.

(France's World War II concentration camps are a difficult subject for both the French and French Jews. But in the last few years some French have begun to acknowledge their nation's complicity in the deportation and murder of their fellow Frenchmen as well as foreign Jews living in France.)

Not far from Paris is the town of Drancy. You may even drive through it on your way to or from Charles de Gaulle Airport. There, in 1941, a transit camp was set up in an unfinished complex of apartment buildings. Under the control of the French police, Drancy was the destination for Jews rounded up by the Germans and their French collaborators during the occupation. From here they were shipped to Auschwitz and other death camps. Most did not return. Conditions in Drancy were dreadful and the French guards brutal. Food was inadequate and thousands of people had to make do with just a few toilets. Prisoners were forced into primitive and overcrowded quarters and were subjected to the kind of degradation that comes with being deprived of basic sanitary necessities. They were kept here for weeks before going to Auschwitz. Children were separated from their parents and sent to Drancy without any care at all. Many died from starvation. And it was to Drancy and Auschwitz that the Jews were sent from the infamous Vél d'Hiv (see above in the 15th Arrondissement section) after the French police rounded them up on the nights of July 16 and 17, 1942.

Chartres

A fine day trip from Paris (about an hour by train from the Gare Montparnasse) is Chartres, with its lovely town and magnificent cathedral, which displays a blend of Gothic and Romanesque architecture. The town is very quaint and is complete with cobblestone streets, ironwork lamps, and timbered houses.

Chartres was a major Christian pilgrimage destination in the Middle Ages because it was the repository of the garment supposedly worn by Mary when she gave birth to Jesus.

One of the cathedral's exquisite twelfth-century stained-glass windows depicts the Passion of Jesus, and in that window you will see a good example of Ecclesia and Synagoga. Here, Synagoga is permanently blinded by a devil in the form of a beast.

Chartres's rue des Juifs was located to the right of the cathedral, near the river, until the early 1970s.

Other *Paris* Resources

JEWISH CENTER

La Maison France-Israël. 64, avenue Marceau.
Tel: 01-44-43-36-00.

> Not far from the Arc de Triomphe, this relatively new institution is very receptive to the needs of American tourists, and the friendly staff makes visitors feel at home. Also in the complex are Jewish radio stations, the Simon Wiesenthal Center, the France-Israel Chamber of Commerce, the Alliance France-Israël, and other organizations. The kosher restaurant La Brasserie des Champs (see below) is also here.

CONSISTOIRES

The Consistoire Central and the Consistoire de Paris see to the religious needs of Jews in France. Many officials speak English and Hebrew.

Consistoire Central. 19, rue St.-Georges.
Tel: 01-49-70-88-00.

Consistoire de Paris. 17, rue St.-Georges.
Tel: 01-40-82-26-26.

OTHER SYNAGOGUES

The synagogues listed at the end of each arrondissement section are all under the aegis of the Consistoire and are Orthodox. There are a few non-Orthodox synagogues in Paris as well.

Conservative Synagogue

La Communauté Adath Shalom. 8, rue Georges Bernard Shaw. Tel: 01-45-67-97-96.

> Paris's only Conservative synagogue. A number of members are English or American, and many others speak English. All in all, this synagogue has a very welcoming congregation. Call if you are interested in spending Shabbat with them, or if you'd like to have a Shabbat meal with one of the members.

Liberal Synagogues

Many American residents and visitors attend services at the rue Copernic synagogue. Their community Passover seder is partially in English, and there is an English-speaking secretary. (Liberal Judaism is similar to American Reform Judaism.)

Mouvement Juif Libéral de France. 11, rue Gaston de Caillavet. Tel: 01-45-75-38-01.

Union Libérale Israélite de France. 22–24, rue Copernic. Tel: 01-47-04-37-27.

KOSHER RESTAURANTS

Here is a list of kosher restaurants in neighborhoods not described elsewhere in the guide. You'll probably find yourself in at least one of these areas while you are touring Paris. All have Beth Din supervision.

1st Arrondissement

Juliette. 14, rue Duphot. Tel: 01-42-60-18-05 or 01-42-60-18-10.

Meat, French cuisine.

2nd Arrondissement

Dream On Café. 36, rue Vivienne. Tel: 01-42-21-46-30.

Meat, California cuisine. Piano bar.

Ikuma By Yun-Pana. 41, rue d'Aboukir.
Tel: 01-42-21-46-25.

Meat, Japanese.

Ninou. 30, rue Léopold-Bellan. Tel: 01-45-08-05-44.

Meat, traditional Jewish.

Panini Folie. 11, rue du Ponceau. Tel: 01-42-33-14-55.

Dairy.

8th Arrondissement

Cine Citta Café St. Honoré. 7, rue d'Aguesseau.
Tel: 01-42-68-05-03.

Dairy, Italian.

La Brasserie des Champs. La Maison France-Israël.
64, avenue Marceau. Tel: 01-56-62-31-31.

Meat, French cuisine.

Maestro Pizza. 19, rue d'Anjou. Tel: 01-47-42-15-60.

Dairy, Italian.

Sivan. 36, rue de Berri. Tel: 01-49-53-01-21.

Meat, French cuisine.

14th Arrondissement

Pil-El-Café. 209, boulevard Raspail.
Tel: 01-43-21-10-65.

Meat.

17th Arrondissement

Brasserie du Belvédère. 109, avenue de Villiers.
Tel: 01-47-64-96-55.

Meat.

Les Colonnades. 51, rue Bayen. Tel: 01-45-72-08-02.

Dairy, fish.

Nini Japonais. 5, rue Fourcroy. Tel: 01-46-22-10-11.

Meat, Japanese.

CHAPTER THREE

Normandy

Caen

NOTHING REMAINS OF THE medieval Jewish community that existed in Caen, but the city contains a very moving memorial to the tens of thousands of American and Allied soldiers who gave their lives to liberate Europe from the Germans. It is also a good place from which to visit the various D day landing beaches.

SIGHTS

Museum

Musée pour la Paix. Boulevard du Général Eisenhower. Tel: 02-31-06-06-44.

Note the last six digits of the phone number here: 06 (June), 06 (sixth day), 44 (1944)—D day.

D Day Landing Beaches and American Cemetery

There have been dozens of movies made about the D Day landings, but no movie, regardless of how realistic it purports to be, can match the profound sense of humility that overcomes you when you actually see Omaha Beach and Pointe du Hoc.

Immediately above and behind the now clean and tranquil Pointe du Hoc, the countryside is still full of vast, deep bomb craters. German fortifications and gun emplacements are everywhere. Take a walk through them and you can peer into wall openings that held machine guns and mortars, and through the observation points from which the Germans had a clear view to anyone and anything coming close to the beach. They still bear the scorch marks of American flamethrowers and grenades.

Today, it is difficult to fathom what those men were up against, but you can get some sense of what a miracle it was that anyone managed to get off those beaches, let alone prevail in battle. Knowing that the German troop deployment was relatively light because they believed the invasion would be at the Pas de Calais, further up the French coast, does not minimize the fact that the Germans had a clear tactical advantage over those landing on the beach.

Just when you think you've seen everything, you'll get to the American military cemetery at Colleville-sur-Mer. Nothing can prepare you for the endless neat rows of simple white crosses punctuated by white stars of David—thousands and thousands of testaments to what happened on the battlefields you just saw.

Jewish grave from the D Day invasion,
American military cemetery at
Colleville-sur-Mer

Rouen

TODAY'S FAIRLY SMALL JEWISH community goes
back to the eleventh century and perhaps even a bit
before. One of the events that defines Rouen in Jewish history is
that it was one of two towns where Jews were put to death during
the First Crusade (Metz was the other). At the time, though, it was
under English rule and was not part of France.

We know from the rolls of what was called the Normandy
Jewish tax that when Rouen became French again, the community
began to decline. And for over two hundred years there were no
Jews at all in Rouen until the end of the sixteenth century, when a
handful of Conversos came to settle. Conversos owned their own

cemetery and they more than likely observed at least some Jewish laws and customs in private. They practiced Christianity in public, but officials often accused them of practicing Judaism and levied harsh financial penalties. The descendants of the Conversos did not stay in Rouen; they wandered farther afield to places like Amsterdam, Antwerp, Hamburg, and London, so that by the eighteenth century nothing was left of that community.

At the end of the eighteenth century a new community was formed almost entirely of Jews from Alsace. In August 1976, the excavation in and around Rouen's Palais de Justice yielded an unexpected treasure: a yeshiva dating back to the twelfth or thirteenth century, though there is some controversy about just what the building was, a yeshiva or a synagogue. Rouen's Palais de Justice is on the northern boundary of what was the rue des Juifs. French texts from the fifteenth century indicate that this spot was a Jewish school. Known locally today as the Jewish Monument, though it is not actually a monument, it seems very likely that this was the main Normandy yeshiva. It is also believed that a number of great Jewish scholars who, because of previous mistranslation of various manuscripts and documents, were thought to be associated with other yeshivas, may in fact have been associated with a Rouen yeshiva. These include Rabbi Samuel ben Meir (Rashbam) and Abraham ibn Ezra, who wrote extensive commentaries on Exodus (the second book of the Torah), Prophets, and Daniel.

SIGHTS

Old Jewish Quarter

The Jewish quarter of the Middle Ages was known as rue de Gyeus, which became rue des Juifs. The cemetery outside of the city was known as Mont aux Juifs.

Medieval Yeshiva

The Jewish Monument, courtyard of the Palais de Justice. See the paragraph above about the Palais de Justice.

Synagogue

The present synagogue was reconstructed in 1950 on the site of a synagogue built in 1860 and destroyed during World War II. The activities of the present Jewish community, some seven hundred people, are centered here.

Cathedral

Cathédrale de Rouen, place de la Cathédrale. The window to the far right of the apse depicts the story of the relationship between Judaism and Christianity. In this version the Torah (the first five books of what Christians refer to as the Old Testament) was merely a foretelling of the events of the Christian New Testament. The windows portray scenes that, according to this interpretation of biblical events, foretell the rise and triumph of the Christian Church and the downfall of the Synagogue, that is, Judaism. This is similar to the Ecclesia and Synagoga statues that can be seen on many French cathedrals. Here, both are shown as women on opposite sides of the crucified Jesus. Synagoga, her crown tilting on her head, is blindfolded; her staff is broken, her head is bowed in defeat, and a moon in eclipse is over her head. The figure representing the Church is crowned by the sun shining over her head. Judas wears the pointed hat worn by medieval Jews.

Normandy Resources

ROUEN

Synagogue and community center: 55, rue des Bons-Enfants. Tel: 02-35-71-01-44.

Shabbat and festival minyan.

Kosher food: The community center has a kosher food center that is open daily except Saturday. Call for hours.

CAEN

Synagogue: 46/48, avenue de la Libération.
Tel: 02-31-43-60-54.

Daily, Shabbat, and festival minyan.

Kosher grocery: Elie Lasry. 26, rue l'Engannerie.
Tel: 02-31-86-16-25.

DEAUVILLE

Mikvah: 19, rue Castor. Tel: 02-31-81-27-03.

Kosher food: Les Goulettoises. 29 bis, rue Bremey, place du Marché (restaurant under supervision of Beth Din of Paris).

LE HAVRE

Mikvah: Tel: 02-35-42-50-15.

Kosher food: Epicerie Super U Porte Océan. Boulevard François. Tel: 02-35-21-31-25. There is another location: 5, rue A. Périer. Tel: 02-35-21-25-35.

CABOURG

Kosher food: Epicerie Super U. Boulevard Maurice Thorez. Tel: 02-31-19-17-89.

CHAPTER FOUR

Brittany

Brittany has been home to Jews since the fifth century C.E.—albeit very few. Even today the Jewish population remains small. Though there aren't many records, there is documentation of a massacre of Jews by crusaders in 1236. The survivors were thrown out by the local duke, Jean le Roux, in 1240. Not satisfied with just getting rid of the remnant of the Jewish population, he declared debts to Jews to be invalid not only during his rule, but also during the rule of his successors. This may go far to explain why, historically, many of Brittany's Jews converted to Christianity.

The eighteenth century saw some settlement of Jewish traders who came from Bordeaux, Alsace, and Lorraine, but they were expelled in 1780. After the Revolution and the liberalization of Jewish life, Jews once again settled in Nantes, Brest, Rennes, and Saint-Servan.

Le Mans

THIS WAS AN IMPORTANT COMMUNITY in the Middle Ages—one that produced great Jewish scholarship. At the time, Jews lived in the area between rue Marchande, rue Saint Jacques, rue Folotiers, rue Merdereau, rue Barillerie, Pont Neuf, and rue de la Juiverie. The community had its own market, school, and even a hospital. In 1289, the Jews were expelled along with Jews of Maine and Anjou.

Le Mans's Jews, like the rest of the Jews in France, did not fare well during World War II, when many were deported and murdered. The postwar community is largely North African in origin.

SIGHTS

Cathedral

Cathédrale St. Julien, old le Mans quarter, has some stained-glass windows that depict the synagogue.

Deportation Memorial

The deportation memorial cannot be visited independently, so inquire at the synagogue/community center. Tel: 02-43-86-00-96.

Nantes

*T*HIS ALWAYS-SMALL COMMUNITY CAN be traced back to the middle of the thirteenth century, and rue des Juifs marks the place where many Jews lived.

Portuguese Conversos settled here in the mid-sixteenth century, including Abraham d'Espinoza, grandfather of Baruch Spinoza, the Dutch Jewish philosopher who was put in Cherem (banned from contact with other Jews and the Jewish community) for views that were deemed heretical by the rabbis of his time.

The community built a synagogue in 1870, at a time when about fifty families were in residence in the city.

The census taken by the Vichy government counted 531 Jews in Nantes. But by mid-1943 there were only 53. Most were deported and some were imprisoned at the Caserne de Richemont outside town.

SIGHTS

Synagogue

5, Impasse Copernic. Call the synagogue at 02-40-47-48-16 or 02-40-46-42-05 to make arrangements for visiting the 1870 structure.

Brittany *Resources*

LE MANS

Synagogue: 4–6, boulevard Paixhans.
Tel: 02-43-86-00-96.

Services on Shabbat.

NANTES

Synagogue: 5, Impasse Copernic. Tel: 02-40-73-48-92.

Daily and Shabbat minyan.

Mikvah: 5, Impasse Copernic. Tel: 02-40-47-48-16.

Kosher food: Inquire at the synagogue.

CHAPTER FIVE

The Loire Valley

TODAY, THE JEWISH COMMUNITIES in the Loire region are small. The towns of Angers, Blois, and Tours all had medieval Jewish communities, but nothing of them remains.

Angers

THE RUE DE LA Juiverie is not the location of Angers's medieval Jewish community. Though Jews lived here in the twelfth and thirteenth centuries, Charles II tossed them out at the end of the thirteenth. Some returned at the end of the fourteenth century to horrific and violent abuse. The reunification of the region with France in 1390 set the stage for their expulsion along with the rest of France's Jews in 1394.

SIGHTS

Cathédrale St.-Maurice, Place Ste.-Croix

Above the portal there are some Hebrew inscriptions that describe the Messiah.

Blois

THIS TOWN, KNOWN FOR its beautiful château, remains a tainted place in French Jewish history as the site of France's first blood libel accusation. On May 26, 1171, the local count, Theobald, ordered thirty-three Jewish men, women, and children to their deaths at the stake as a punishment for an alleged ritual murder. So horrific was this incident that the rabbis of the day declared the Hebrew date (the twentieth of Sivan) a fast day for Jews in France, England, and the German Rhineland. Blois became known as the City of Blood. Rabbenu Tam, one of Rashi's grandsons, wrote an elegy for the dead of Blois that became incorporated into the liturgy. The atrocity was remembered in the twentieth century in a Hebrew play—*Pulzelinah*, by S. D. Goitein—in 1927.

Jews lived in Blois as early as 992. But today's rue des Juifs, near the cathedral, is probably the site of a mid-fourteenth-century community.

Pithiviers

*I*N 1941, AT A WORLD WAR I military installation, the Germans set up a camp as a holding pen for foreign Jews in France; it was one of two such camps (Beaune-la-Rolande, southeast of Pithiviers, was the other). Though most Jews were sent to Auschwitz from the Paris suburb of Drancy, there were some deportations from Pithiviers—mostly of Jews from southern France. Some sixteen thousand Jews were deported from Pithiviers and Beaune-la-Rolande. Though the camp no longer remains, a memorial was dedicated in 1957.

SIGHTS

Monument

Monument aux Israélites, Square Max Jacob. Close to the side of the railroad tracks, and near the present Parc Municipal des Sports, is what is left of the camp from which several thousand Jews were sent to their deaths in the German death camps. Jews were imprisoned here beginning in May 1941, and beginning in 1943 members of the French Resistance were also imprisoned. The camp was liberated on August 9, 1944. After the war the camp was razed and the land sold.

Tours

*T*OURS IS VERY OLD in terms of French Jewish history. Historians have evidence of Jewish life here as far back as the late sixth century. In the Middle Ages, Jews lived in an area near the rue de la Caserne. They had a synagogue and leased a plot of land from a local archbishop for use as a cemetery (near the rue du Cygne). In it they were required to bury not only their own dead, but also Jews from other places. The Jewish community of Tours ceased to exist for all intents and purposes until the 1970s, when immigrants from North Africa revitalized it.

SIGHTS

Cathedral

The Cathédrale St. Gatien, place de la Cathédrale (near the Musée des Beaux Arts), has a thirteenth-century stained-glass window depicting a Jew striking the statue of St. Nicholas.

Loire Resources

ANGERS

Synagogue: 12, rue Valdemaine. Tel: 02-41-87-48-10.
Shabbat minyan.

Kosher food: For information contact the synagogue.

TOURS

Synagogue: 37, rue Parmentier. Tel: 02-47-05-56-95.
Shabbat minyan; Thursday morning minyan.

Community center: 6, rue Chalmel. Tel: 02-47-05-59-07.

CHAPTER SIX

Poitou-Charentes

THIS REGION OF FRANCE HAS A limited Jewish history that does not reach much beyond the Middle Ages. At the time, there were communities in cities like Poitiers, and numerous cities and towns in the region, such as Montaigu, Niort, and La Rochelle, still have street and place-names like La Juderie and rue de la Juiverie.

In the mid-twelfth century Jews arrived in Poitou from Narbonne in the south, and there were a few Poitou Jewish scholars who were part of the renowned Synod of Troyes organized by Shmuel ben Meir and Jacob ben Meir Tam.

Poitou was under English rule briefly in the early thirteenth century and during that time the English kings protected the Jews. When Poitou reverted to France in 1224, local Jews suffered attacks by the crusaders. The ruler, Alphonse of Poitiers, expelled Poitou's Jews in 1268 (in an effort to finance his participation in the Crusades), but not before he imprisoned them, seized their property, and exacted a high ransom for their release. When they were allowed back briefly they were required to wear a special badge.

By 1270 Poitou had been incorporated into France, and though France as a whole did not expel the Jews until 1306, Poitou saw to their expulsion in 1291. Some returned in 1315 only to be accused of being lepers.

CHAPTER SEVEN

Aquitaine and the Basque Country

Settlements of Jews have been in this region since the fourth century, and Bordeaux and Agen were the primary places of Jewish residence. But this has been a historically volatile area, sitting as it does between France and Spain, and Jews lived here not only at the sufferance of the French monarch, but at the whim of the British one as well, because this area was ruled by England from 1152 to 1453.

Expulsions were the norm, as were Jewish taxes and forfeiture of Jewish property to one crown or the other. And it was here in 1320 that the Pastoureaux (Shepherds), crusaders against the Muslims in Spain, massacred thousands of Jews as well as others. Bordeaux's local lord finally stopped them in their rampage throughout southwestern France.

Agen

AS EARLY AS 1263, documents indicate special taxes levied upon the Jews of Agen, to be paid to the local bishop. Jews returning to Agen following the general expulsion of 1306 were massacred by the Pastoureaux in 1320.

SIGHTS

Old Jewish Quarter

Ancient ghetto, rue des Juifs. Circa 1342.

Museum

Deportation Museum. 28, rue Montesquieu (same location as synagogue and community center)
Tel: 05-53-48-29-17.

Matzo Bakery

S. Bitone, Père et Fils. Rue Michelet.

Bayonne

CONVERSOS FROM SPAIN AND Portugal first settled in the Bayonne suburb of Saint Esprit in the sixteenth century, when they were given residency permits as New Christians.

They were not, however, permitted to engage in retail trade. Some of these refugees were expelled in 1636 and settled in Nantes.

The community was formally established in the mid-seventeenth century. Calling themselves Nefuzot Yehudah (the Dispersed of Judah), they founded a cemetery in 1660, but their right to practice Judaism in the open did not come until 1723. By 1753, some thirty-five hundred Jews lived in Bayonne.

After the June 1940 armistice that divided France into occupied and unoccupied zones, Bayonne was a stopping point for Jews fleeing Belgium and Luxembourg, hoping to get to relative safety in Spain. In April 1943, the Jews of Bayonne and the surrounding area were deported, and few, either native French or refugee, survived the war. The community rebuilt itself after the war, and today about one thousand Jews, mostly Sephardim, call it home. The chocoholics among us can thank the Jews of Bayonne for their role in introducing the manufacture of chocolate to France.

SIGHTS

Synagogue

35, rue Maubec. Tel: 05-59-55-03-95. Built in 1837.

Museum

Basque Museum. 1, rue Marengo. Tel: 05-59-59-08-98.
The Louis XVI–style ark and some of the Torah scrolls were hidden in the Basque museum during the war.

Cemeteries

There are a number of very old cemeteries in the area. There's one in Bidache, with headstones from 1690. There are two in

Peyrehorade: one on rue des Chapons, in the center of town, has headstones from 1628, and the other has headstones from 1737. There's yet another at Labastide-Clairence. To visit any of the cemeteries inquire at 05-59-55-03-95.

Bordeaux

*T*HERE ARE INDICATIONS THAT Jews lived in Bordeaux as early as the fourth century C.E., though written evidence goes back only to the sixth century.

Ruled by England from 1154 until 1253, Bordeaux's Jews did not suffer from the same expulsions from the French kingdom as did their brethren. Nonetheless, they were subject to anti-Jewish measures imposed upon them by the English Crown in the form of high taxes and special Jewish tariffs. In 1320, during the Pastoureaux uprisings, the Jews of Bordeaux suffered greatly at the hands of violent mobs.

Conversos fleeing the inquisition in Spain and Portugal began to settle in Bordeaux at the end of the fifteenth century, and in 1550, permits from King Henry II granted these "Portuguese New Christians" the right to settle in whichever towns they chose. This largesse on the part of the king was not unrelated to the Jews' talent for business. And though many residents suspected them of not really being the practicing Catholics they claimed to be, the authorities left them alone. Indeed, one can wonder how much the local Church authorities did know, given that in 1710 the New Christians were granted their own section of one of the parish cemeteries. It was during that same year that they began to be a bit more open about their Jewish origins. But it was not until 1723, in an application for a new set of permits, that these Portuguese merchants were first referred to openly as Jews. But by that time, Jews in name as well as practice had started arriving from Avignon and other areas of Comtat Venaissin. By 1753, though practicing Judaism in public was still against the law, the Jews of Bordeaux gathered for prayer in some seven private locations.

During this period, the Jewish community supported its own community enterprises such as doctors for the poor, circumcisions, grave diggers, and weddings. In addition they raised money for the support of Jews in the four holy communities of Israel (Jerusalem, Safed, Tiberias, and B'nai B'rak).

At the dawn of the eighteenth century, Bordeaux was home to 1,422 Jews of Portuguese origin and 348 Jews from the Comtat Venaissin. In 1734, 1740, and 1748 expulsion orders were issued, but each time the community found a way to have their stay extended. And by 1759 six families from Avignon were granted letters patent to settle.

The community of Bordeaux sent a delegation of two, Abraham Furtado and S. Lopes-Dubec, to the committee led by Minister to the French Crown Chrétien de Malesherbes, who was, just prior to the start of the French Revolution, investigating civil rights for French Jews. Furtado, along with Isaac Rodrigues, was also a delegate from the department of the Gironde to Napoleon's Assembly of Jewish Notables convened in 1806, and Lopes-Dubec went on to represent the Gironde in the National Assembly in 1848.

During the nineteenth century, Jews played an important role in the municipal, commercial, and intellectual affairs of Bordeaux and the department in general. It was during this time that Baron Nathaniel de Rothschild, of the English branch of the family, founded the winery Château Mouton Rothschild in the Médoc (1853), and his cousin Baron James founded Château Lafite Rothschild (1867). The year 1882 saw the consecration of the Great Synagogue of Bordeaux.

Thousands of Jews fleeing the German occupation in the north of France came to Bordeaux in May and June 1940. But by June 21, 1940, the date of the Franco-German armistice which put Bordeaux into the occupied zone, that would prove dangerous, as

Bordeaux became a center of Nazi activity. Two-thirds of all Jews were deported to the death camps. True to Nazi cruelty and love of irony, the Great Synagogue was used as a detention center for Jews waiting to be deported, and homegrown French fascists vandalized the synagogue in January 1944.

At war's end the Bordeaux community was all but destroyed, but the few survivors undertook a rebuilding of their synagogue. By 1960 the population was up to three thousand, and immigrants from North Africa nearly doubled that by 1970. Today's population remains fairly constant and most are the descendants of families who arrived after World War II. The vast majority are Sephardim, with a sprinkling of Ashkenazim.

SIGHTS

Access to the various Jewish monuments can be obtained by calling the Secrétariat of the Consistoire at 05-56-91-79-39.

Synagogue

Rue du Grand-Rabbin Joseph-Cohen. Built in 1882, Bordeaux's first large synagogue replaced another built in 1810 and destroyed by fire in 1873. Prior to its construction, the community used several private prayer rooms. This huge, fifteen-hundred-seat building, with its columns of Carrara marble, is the largest synagogue in France. During the occupation, French fascists destroyed much of the interior before the Germans turned it into a detention center for Jews being shipped to death camps further east. It was restored after the war.

Ghetto

Not much remains, but remnants can be seen on the rue Cheverus just off the Ste. Catherine pedestrian mall. It was once known as Arrua Judega. If you make a left turn onto rue de la Porte Dijeaux you will come to the city gate once known as Jews' Gate.

Cemeteries

74, cours de la Marne. Founded in 1725.

Cours de l'Yser, seventeenth century. Note that Pauline and Hans Herzl, children of Theodor Herzl, the founder of modern political Zionism, are buried here.

Churches

The Church of St.-Seurin, place des Martyrs de la Résistance. On the left side of the south portal you can see a statue of Synagoga.

Street Names

A number of Bordeaux's streets are named for noted Jews: rue David Gradis, a shipping magnate; rue (Abraham) Furtado, chairman of Napoleon's Assembly of Jewish Notables and treasurer of Bordeaux; avenue Georges Mandel, minister of the interior, assassinated in 1944; and several streets are named for Léon Blum, former prime minister of France.

Pau

SIGHTS

Synagogue

8, rue des Trois-Frères-Bernadac. Tel: 05-59-62-37-85. Built around 1850.

Concentration Camps

Nearby at Gurs is the site of one of France's largest concentration camps. Though the French are loath to admit to camps on French soil, this was one of several. Conditions here were horrific and deemed worse than in the camps in occupied France. Some eight hundred Jews died here during the winter of 1940. In 1941, seventy-two hundred Jewish deportees from Germany were imprisoned here, along with three thousand Jews who were first arrested in Belgium and then sent to the camp at St. Cyprien before coming to Gurs. In July 1942, following an inspection by one of Adolf Eichmann's deputies, the Gurs inmates were moved to Drancy outside Paris and then to death camps. The camp cemetery contains the graves of twelve hundred Jews.

Aquitaine Resources

AGEN

Synagogue and community center: 52, rue de Montesquieu. Tel: 05-53-48-29-17.

Shabbat and festival minyan.

Kosher food: Inquire at community center.

BAYONNE

Synagogue and community center: 35, rue Maubec. Tel: 05-59-55-03-95.

BORDEAUX

Synagogue: 8, rue du Grand-Rabbin Joseph-Cohen.
Tel: 05-56-91-79-39.

Daily morning and evening minyan; Shabbat and festival minyan.

Mikvah: 213, rue Ste. Catherine. Tel: 05-56-91-64-23.

Kosher restaurant: Mazal Tov. 137, cours Victor Hugo.
Tel: 05-56-52-37-03. Supervision Beth Din of Bordeaux,

Meat. Delivers.

CHAPTER EIGHT

Languedoc-Roussillon

J EWS HAVE A LONG HISTORY IN this region and the number of sites dating from the Middle Ages attests to that. The town of Agde was probably the first place of Jewish settlement as documents dating from as far back as the sixth century demonstrate.

By the Middle Ages, Jews could be found in places like Narbonne, Montpellier, Toulouse, Béziers, Carcassonne, Pamiers, and Lunel. In contrast to the other areas of France, in Languedoc Jews could own real estate and hold public office. But in the thirteenth century, following the Albigensian War and the conquering of Languedoc by France, that all changed, and they became subject to the same punitive taxes, laws, and restrictions as their brethren. The Albigenses were Christian heretics who were friendly toward the Jews. Popular myth held that Judaism influenced their beliefs, but that wasn't true. But the myth was so strong that it prompted the Church to act with even greater hostility toward the Jews, and during the massacres of the Albigenses, Jews too were murdered—particularly in 1209 in Béziers.

The 1306 order that expelled the Jews from France brought

them to Provence, Catalonia (in Spain), and Roussillon—especially Perpignan. It also resulted in the seizure of Jewish property by the French Crown. Local lords opposed this, figuring it would decrease the taxes they themselves could get from their new subjects, but they relented once the Crown gave them a two-thirds share of the property.

A return to France and to Languedoc in 1315 was no blessing. In 1320, the expansion of a movement known as the Pastoureaux resulted in the massacre of thousands of Jews. The Pastoureaux, or Shepherds, were crusaders against the Muslims in Spain who were attempting the rescue of the French king. The movement originated in Picardy in 1251 with a man known as the Master of Hungary (name unknown) who claimed to have been ordered by the Virgin Mary to wage war against the infidels. He and his thirty thousand young followers attacked Jews in Bourges and were subsequently disbanded by the Gascon lord.

But the movement did not die; it only became more popular in this region. This time, the enemy was not only the Muslims in Spain, but also the rich and the clergy. Were it not for the threats against the non-Jewish rich and the Catholic clergy, no attempts would have been made to protect the threatened Jews. In need of weapons, the Pastoureaux murdered Jews to steal their money, but they soon began to slaughter those who refused to be baptized. The massacres were particularly intense in Toulouse, where the Pastoureaux were assisted by local supporters who attacked the Jewish quarter and murdered any Jew who refused baptism. Many Jews in the region committed suicide rather than submit. Eventually the Pastoureaux were repressed by the viscount of Toulouse and King James of Aragon, who had many of them killed.

Contemporary Jews chronicled the Pastoureaux massacres. According to eyewitness accounts, some 120 communities suffered during the carnage, and those who were forced to accept baptism on pain of death were not permitted to reembrace Judaism by order of the inquisition.

The Jews of Languedoc moved around constantly, the result of one expulsion order after another. In 1395, following the decree of 1394, many left for Comtat Venaissin and Provence. By the end of the eighteenth century Jews had settled again in Narbonne, Toulouse, and Nîmes without incident or opposition.

The Roussillon region was home to numerous Jewish scholars who were distinguished not only in religious pursuits, but in the secular intellectual realm as well. Perpignan, in which nothing of the medieval community remains, was a Tosafist center. Jewish physicians were well known and served towns all over the area. Many studied at the University of Montpellier in the fourteenth century.

Béziers

KNOWN AS LA PETITE Jérusalem (Little Jerusalem) during the Middle Ages, Béziers was a center of Jewish learning and the home to many Jewish scholars, poets, and liturgists. Among those were Abraham ibn Ezra (1089–1164), who wrote Torah commentaries and structural works on the Hebrew language, and Benjamin of Tudela, the twelfth-century traveler who chronicled the Jewish world of his day. The Jews of Béziers were massacred during the bloody Albigensian War in 1209.

SIGHTS

Ghetto

Ancient ghetto of Pézenas. This fourteenth-century ghetto is still pretty much intact. Located just under the walls of the castle, it can be seen between the Faugères and Biaise gates. Entry is through a low archway that leads to the rue de la Juiverie and goes up to the rue Litanie—known as the careyra de las litanias. Stones from the ancient synagogue can be seen in the cloister of the St. Nazaire cathedral. For additional information on visits to the ghetto contact Mr. Benyacar of the Jewish community in Béziers, tel: 04-67-31-14-23, or the local tourism office, place Gambetta, Pézenas, tel: 04-67-98-11-82.

Montpellier

THIS WAS A SIGNIFICANT Jewish community in the Middle Ages because it was home to several yeshivas. The city's medieval Jewish quarter was located around the present rue de la Barralerie (see the Sights section below).

The Jews of Montpellier were a relatively prosperous group and earned their living initially as tradesmen and merchants. Money lending did not become a primary occupation until the thirteenth century. In addition, they were also involved in the supply of weapons during times of war. When money lending did fall to the Jews, they were subject to a complex regulatory system that served to partially protect them from some of the excesses prevalent in other localities.

Montpellier was home to a number of Jewish physicians. Though some sources say that medieval Jews had a hand in the establishment of the city's famous medical school, other sources disagree. However, a number of Jewish names can be found on the school's entranceway pediments. In addition to many physicians, the town was home to scholars and poets such as Aryeh Judah Harari (a liturgical poet) and the physician-philosopher Abraham Avigdor, who wrote medical as well as philosophical and literary treatises.

Jewish residence in Montpellier during the Middle Ages was often at the whim of the local lord and dependent on the political situation and disputes over property between the kings of Majorca and the king of France. And when they weren't being fought over by the monarchs, the local Christians could force the Jews to move from one quarter to another. The building of a synagogue in 1387 resulted in a lawsuit against the Jewish community and judgment to the plaintiff in the amount of four hundred livres—a huge sum. In addition, Jews were forced to supply the money and the manpower for the town's defense, especially in the mid-fourteenth century. The general expulsion from France in 1394 was preceded by much rancor against the Jews on the part of local officials.

In later centuries Montpellier was home to Conversos from Spain and Portugal and traders from Comtat Venaissin. But even by the eighteenth century, Jewish residence here was strictly regulated, and at the beginning of the twentieth century it was home to only about thirty-five families.

After the 1940 agreement with the Germans, Montpellier found itself in unoccupied France, and as such it became a haven for Jews fleeing other parts of the country. It maintained this role even after this part of France was occupied by the Germans, when it became a center for Jewish partisans.

The community of today is largely of North African origin and has a number of synagogues and Jewish communal organizations.

SIGHTS

Mikvah

Under the city walls at 1, rue de la Barralerie, the entrance to the medieval Jewish quarter, is a thirteenth-century mikvah that has been restored. You can visit this vaulted series of rooms and see its staircase, the disrobing room, the actual bath, and even the water. For visits contact the Office of Tourism: Le Triangle. 78, avenue du Pirée. Tel: 04-67-58-67-58.

Languedoc-Roussillon Resources

BÉZIERS

Synagogue: 19, place Pierre-Sémard.
Tel: 04-67-28-75-98.

Shabbat minyan.

Mikvah: 19, place Pierre-Sémard. Tel: 04-67-28-44-24.

Kosher food: Inquire at the synagogue.

MONTPELLIER

Synagogue: 7, rue Général Laffon. Tel: 04-67-92-92-07.

Daily morning and evening minyan; Shabbat and festival minyan.

Mikvah: 45, rue Proudhon. Tel: 04-67-72-49-17.

Kosher food: Inquire at the synagogue.

$\mathcal{P}$rovence

$\mathcal{P}$ROVENCE IS A GOLD MINE OF French and European Jewish history—a real find for the tourist interested in Jewish sites and French Jewish heritage.

The area that we know today as Provence has had Jewish communities since the first century C.E., though evidence is scarce. Archaeological data place communities in fifth-century Arles and sixth-century Marseille. It is in Provence, and the neighboring region of Languedoc-Roussillon, that we find some of the oldest Jewish sites in France. The area referred to throughout this book as Comtat Venaissin, the papal administrative area, and a key geographical region for French Jewish history, is in Provence in the department of the Vaucluse.

By the middle of the fourteenth century, the Jewish population in Provence had reached nearly fifteen thousand. Jews could be found in the towns and cities of Aix-en-Provence, Draguignan, Fréjus, Grasse, Saint-Rémy, Toulon, and about eighty other places.

Documentation from Arles tells us something about local Jewish community administration in the thirteenth century. In addition to the usual Jewish charitable organizations and educational societies, there was a government-mandated organization that was responsible for collecting the special Jew tax payable to the ruler of Provence.

The Provençal Jews earned a living as small moneylenders and business brokers. They didn't have the kind of capital necessary to make large commercial loans; that end of the business was in Christian hands, though there were a few Jewish families in it, too. Wheat and wine made up most of their brokerage enterprises, and some Jews also dealt in textiles and real estate. There were also a large number of Jewish doctors.

Jewish literature and scholarship thrived in Provence, and the region was renowned as a center of this in the medieval world. Ruled by the Carolingians (see the beginning of chapter 1 for a discussion of them) and without much contact with the Jews in Muslim Spain (another medieval center of Jewish literature and scholarship), Provence was influenced by German Jewry and the communities of northern France. The Jewish scholars of Provence studied and interpreted the Talmud with uncommon skill and creativity. All of Jewish Europe, apart from Spain, sought them out for their knowledge and facility with halacha (Jewish law). The scholars of Provence dispensed their knowledge in the form of oral law as opposed to the written law prevalent in some other Jewish traditions. They also created midrashim (new meanings in the text of the Torah) and minhagim (customs and observances), and developed new interpretations of earlier midrashim.

The twelfth century saw a melding of Provençal Jewish culture and scholarship with that of Barcelona Jewry when parts of Provence came under the rule of Catalonia. As a result, the intellectual life of both communities grew richer and more complex. The Provençal Jews moved from their concentration on the Talmud and began to include sciences, poetry, and philosophy in their scholarly repertoire. They also embraced the translation of Arabic literature into Hebrew. They did all this without diminishing their expertise in halacha. Provençal scholars included Rabbi Moshe of Arles and his son Rabbi Judah ben Moshe of Arles, whose Talmudic interpretations are cited in some of Rashi's work; Gershon ben Shlomo of Arles, author of *Sh'ar HaShamayim,* a work of metaphysics; and Nissim ben Moshe of Marseille, author of *Ma'seh Nissim,* a book of miracle stories taken from Talmudic sources.

The social and economic fortunes of Provence's Jews changed with each successive local lord, count, and bishop. And there were some very good times as well as difficult ones. Whereas Charles of Anjou (1246–85) limited the amount of control the Spanish Inquisition had over the Jews in his domain, Charles II (1285–1309) issued numerous anti-Jewish regulations taken directly from the inquisition: Jews could not employ Christians, Jews could not hold public office, Jews had to wear a special badge, and so on. King Robert (1309–45) was both good and bad. He helped Jews collect debts owed to them and he refused to expel the Jews despite pressure by the Catholic clergy to do so. But he saw to it that Jews lived in segregated quarters—sometimes in entirely separate Jewish towns.

Provence was no stranger to anti-Jewish riots, particularly in the fourteenth century. The worst and the most infamous took place in Toulon in 1348 at the height of the Black Death when the Jewish community was almost completely wiped out. The loss of life was so extreme that Queen Jeanne (1343–82) lowered the special Jew tax for ten years.

Things got considerably better in the fifteenth century: Queen Yolande protected the Jews from the whim of local magistrates, who in other places could arrest and imprison a Jew for no reason at all. In Provence no one could accuse a Jew of something without identifying himself. And Jews without the means to post bail could not be imprisoned unless the charge was one for which the penalty was physical punishment. King René renewed Queen Yolande's favorable regulations, and in 1454 he granted Jews the right to enter any profession or trade, including public office. Jews now had to wear a smaller badge than was previously required, but only in their home territory. The king was also vocal about his opposition to forced baptism and instituted penalties against those who engaged in it.

When King René died in 1481, Provence was united with France. Now, remember that the Jews had been expelled from France in 1394. Despite this, Jews were allowed to remain and continue to enjoy the privileges they had under the previous regime. But before long, in 1484, brutal anti-Jewish violence broke out all over Provence, instigated by local farmworkers and the Franciscan and Carmelite clergies. The teenaged king of France, Charles VIII, protected the Jews as best he could, but he was unable to end the mayhem. As a result, Jews began to leave Provence for other areas, but the violence was so disruptive that town after town called for their expulsion. By 1498, King Louis XII issued a general expulsion order, though it was not enforced until 1501.

The issuance of an expulsion order left Jews without much choice—pack up and move or convert to Christianity. Sadly, some Jews chose the latter. But sometimes even conversion wasn't enough to stem social and economic isolation. Jews who converted but remained in Provence had to pay a special tax to compensate the Crown for the loss of the regular Jew tax, known as the neophyte tax. Records from 1512 show that between 122 and 164 heads of families in Provence were subject to it.

During the seventeenth and eighteenth centuries, Jews attempted to resettle in Provence with little success. Local town parliaments permitted Jews to enter their jurisdictions to trade, but not to live.

Note to the Reader

THERE ARE DOZENS OF towns and cities in Provence in which Jews lived at some point during the last several centuries. Most have little or no trace of that community. But you may very well come across street names like rue de la Juiverie, rue des Juifs, or some other name that indicates a Jewish presence at one time. I have only included in this guide those towns that, in addition to having a Jewish history, also have some site of interest to the tourist. In a few instances, because of its tremendous importance in Jewish history, a town will have an entry even though there is nothing of specific Jewish interest to see.

Seeing Jewish Provence

THE BEST WAY TO see the main Jewish sights of Provence is to use Avignon as a base and rent a car, though places are accessible by bus from Avignon's station. Avignon is three hours by train from Paris on one of the speedy TGVs (trains à grande vitesse—high-speed trains). Carpentras is about thirty to forty minutes northeast of Avignon on Route D942, and Cavaillon is thirty to forty minutes southeast on Route D973. Route D49 runs between Carpentras and Cavaillon, and both cities can be easily seen in one day.

Nîmes is about ninety minutes southwest of Avignon on Route N100 and then the A9 motorway; Arles is about ninety minutes southwest on Route N100; Aix-en-Provence is about two hours southeast on Route N7; and Marseille is about three and a half hours southeast also on Route N7. The roads are well marked and easy to navigate, but you will have to get a good map. Michelin no. 245 is a good start, but you may even want something more detailed if you want to avoid highways in favor of a more scenic route.

Avignon and Nice are a considerable distance from each other. If you are spending time in Provence and want to see both areas, it would be best to divide your trip into at least two parts.

Comtat Venaissin

THE GEOGRAPHICAL AREA REFERRED to as Comtat Venaissin corresponds roughly to the present Vaucluse department. It was transferred to the Vatican in 1274 and remained in the hands of the papacy until it was given back to France in 1791. Jews settled in Comtat around the twelfth century, with the exception of Avignon, which had earlier settlements. Comtat Venaissin's major Jewish communities were in the towns of Avignon, Carpentras, Cavaillon, and L'Isle-sur-la-Sorgue, and they were known collectively as the four holy communities. With the exception of L'Isle-sur-la-Sorgue, where no remnant of the medieval community remains, those cities contain some fine vestiges of the Jewish quarters of old.

Because it was separate from France, Comtat Venaissin became a haven for Jews after the various expulsions. Jews in the Comtat spoke a Judeo-Provençal dialect (a mixture of the Hebrew and the Provençal languages) and developed their own liturgy, known as Comtadin.

Avignon

THE ARRIVAL OF JEWS in Avignon is said to date from the first century, after the destruction of the Second Temple in Jerusalem (70 C.E.), but most evidence of Jewish life here dates back only to the twelfth century. Though there is little evidence, Jews have lived around the Jewish quarter since the beginning of their sojourn in Avignon.

The first carrière (the name given to the Jewish quarters of southern France—similar to ghetto) faced the Palace of the Popes on and around the rue de la Vieille Juiverie (old Jewry street). By the early thirteenth century, it was centered on the present rue Jacob and place Jérusalem, where the synagogue stands.

In 1348, Avignon, along with other parts of this region, came under the control of the pope. This represented a turning point for the Jews of France, as Provence and especially the towns of Avignon, Carpentras, Cavaillon, and L'Isle-sur-la-Sorgue became places of refuge from France's many expulsion orders.

The synagogue you see now was built in 1846 to replace a much older one that burned the year before. There were many restrictions on Jewish life within the carrière; walls surrounded the quarter and three gates restricted Jewish comings and goings. Tolls had to be paid to the local Church of St. Peter, and it was forbidden to sell kosher meat outside the carrière. This tiny area, barely one hundred square yards, was home to over one thousand people.

Today's Jewish community is a mix of Sephardim and Ashkenazim, but Sephardim predominate. They number about six hundred families.

SIGHTS

Old Jewish Quarter

Carrière (old Jewish quarter). Rue de la Vieille Juiverie, next to the Palace of the Popes, place Jérusalem.

Synagogue

Place Jérusalem. Tel: 04-90-85-21-24. Reconstructed in 1846 on the site of a thirteenth-century synagogue. Services daily, holidays, and Shabbat. This synagogue, like virtually every other synagogue in France, is Orthodox.

Matzo Bakery

The matzo bakery is next to the synagogue.

Carpentras

J EWS HAVE LIVED HERE on and off since the twelfth century, mostly as refugees from various expulsions. Historical
records show that they were forced to pay the usual Jewish taxes,
and they also show that there were disagreements about who had
jurisdiction over them—the local bishop or the pope (who was
given control of the city by the king of France in 1274).

By the fourteenth century, so many Jews had arrived as
refugees that the local authorities became alarmed and forced the
Jews out of town and destroyed the synagogue. Just to put things
in perspective, a 1473 census indicates approximately 298 Jews living in Carpentras.

In 1343, with some ninety families in residence in the rue
Fournaque near the town walls, the community was permitted to
build a new synagogue and to secure land for a cemetery. A 1459
riot caused the death of sixty people. Soon after, the Jews were
forced to move to the rue de la Muse, which was gated at both
ends and which would become the carrière. Documents of the
time indicate that, apart from money lending, brokerage and agriculture were the primary Jewish occupations.

In the centuries that followed, various constraints were
imposed on the Jews of Carpentras in order to restrict economic
activity and keep Jews and Christians from mixing. By the late sixteenth century, emigration and expulsions had seen the community dwindle, and by the late seventeenth century the population
was down to eighty-three Jewish families. The reduced size of the

community did not prevent continued pressure on Jews to limit the ways they earned a living. Many guilds of the eighteenth century petitioned the local bishop to impose such restrictions.

The desire to restrict Jewish commerce notwithstanding, the city had no qualms about forcing the Jewish community to loan it money when French soldiers occupied Comtat Venaissin from 1746 to 1758. The Jewish community as a whole was far from rich and their debts were very high; more than half of the 160 families were in terrible financial condition. There were of course some very wealthy people, but they were in the minority.

In 1782 some two thousand Jews lived in Carpentras—the community would never get larger. By the time of the French Revolution the Jewish population had dwindled to fewer than seven hundred. Most had left and gone to other towns in the region.

Though the Revolution sowed the seeds of change for Jews in France, those changes were not evident in Carpentras, at least not early on. Pressure to convert to Christianity was still a big problem, and Jews went out of their way not to antagonize local Christians—even going so far as to abstain from voting in elections. When some of the laws did change, as in the case of the requirement to wear yellow hats, Jews were so afraid of the Christian reaction that they stuck with their old garb.

The general antireligious sentiment of the Revolution found its way to Carpentras, too, and in 1794 the Jews agreed to close the synagogue, just as churches all over France had been closed.

Once the revolutionary fervor died down, the Carpentras synagogue reopened in 1800. But by that time, the community had become even smaller, and in 1811, there were just 360 Jews. The Napoleonic edict erasing debts owed to Jews left an already poor community in even worse shape. In the first decades of the twentieth century, services in Carpentras were held only on Yom Kippur—the Day of Atonement. On the eve of World War II barely two dozen families remained. Today's community, mostly elderly Jews, numbers a few hundred people.

SIGHTS

Synagogue

Place de la Maire. Tel: 04-90-63-39-97. Services on holidays and Shabbat only.

Partially restored in 1930, 1953, and 1959, this is a French government–designated historical site. It was originally built between 1741 and 1743 and includes pieces of the fourteenth-century synagogue.

Because of a law forbidding exterior decoration and large size, the exterior is quite plain and is similar to the surrounding houses. But once in the sanctuary you will see that what was forbidden on the outside was not on the inside.

The ornate interior, like the interior of Cavaillon's synagogue (see the Cavaillon section below), is in the rococo style of the eighteenth century. Both synagogues are similar in style to Italian synagogues of the same period. The bimah (the place where the Torah is read and from which services are conducted) and the ark (in which the Torah scrolls are kept) at opposite ends of the room characterize this style, as does the raised bimah.

Note, too, the size of the interior of the ark. It has room for many Torahs. This is typical of synagogues in Europe where old and no-longer-usable Torahs are kept alongside the one in use.

As in all Orthodox synagogues, the women are seated separately from the men. Here the women's section is above in a gallery. But in the older synagogue, the women sat in the basement and had to hear the service through a small window. To facilitate this, there was an official known as the rabbi of women.

The basement of the present structure contains the remnants of a matzo bakery, complete with its preparation table and brick oven built into a wall, and a mikvah. But as restoration is ongoing and occasional, and the basement structures were, at the time of

Synagogue interior, Carpentras

this writing and for the foreseeable future, somewhat unsafe, you will have to secure an appointment to see them.

Cathedral

Cathédrale de St.-Siffrein. The south door of the cathedral, off the rue Mercière, was known as La Porte Juive (Jews' door). Here, in the Middle Ages, Jews were forced to stand outside so they could be preached to.

Cemetery

The medieval cemetery was destroyed after the Jews were expelled from Carpentras in 1322. Its grave markers were used in the construction of the town's ramparts. The present cemetery

Mikvah in Carpentras synagogue basement

was established in 1367, but unfortunately there are no tombstones from that era because they were forbidden by papal edict. The earliest stones are from the eighteenth century. For visits, contact the synagogue (see above in this Sights section).

In May 1990 this cemetery gained a lot of notoriety when it was vandalized by members of the anti-Semitic (and anti–everything else not French) Front National (National Front). One body was taken out of its grave and impaled on a beach umbrella. Some of the anti-Semitic markings can still be seen. Four of the five vandals, "skinheads" in their twenties, were arrested following a confession, tried, and sentenced to twenty months in prison. The fifth was killed in a motorcycle accident.

Cavaillon

*B*EGINNING IN THE MID-FIFTEENTH century, Jews were required to live on the rue Hébraïque, just off the town's main street. But the community itself goes back to the thirteenth century. Though quite a small group, the Jews of Cavaillon were still subject to attack and withstood such popular onslaughts on more than one occasion.

The community gradually got smaller and smaller as the result of emigration—forty-nine Jews in 1811; eight in 1935—and except for some refugees during World War II there were eventually no Jews in Cavaillon until a few from North Africa arrived in the 1960s.

The synagogue you see today is a French historical monument. A sixteenth-century synagogue was integrated into this structure, which itself dates from 1772. The adjacent matzo bakery is now the Musée Judéo-Comtadin.

SIGHTS

Synagogue

Above a passageway between the rue Hébraïque and the rue Chabran, the synagogue overlooks the old carrière. It is smaller than the Carpentras synagogue, but no less ornate. This is no longer a working synagogue, but it is a French historical monument.

Museum

Musée Judéo-Comtadin, in the synagogue's basement (street level), contains remnants of the community's matzo bakery as well as items depicting the community's history—Torah scrolls and

Entrance to Cavaillon ghetto, rue Hébraïque

other ritual objects, historical documents, and so on. Though small, it is a fascinating look at French Jewish life in the town and in the region. For visits to both the synagogue and the museum call 04-90-76-00-34.

Marseille

TODAY, FRANCE'S SECOND LARGEST city is home to France's second largest Jewish community. But Jews have called Marseille home since the sixth century, when an already existing community provided refuge to Jews fleeing forced conversions in Clermont-Ferrand—though things were not much better on that score in Marseille. The Jews of Marseille were scholars, merchants, laborers, coral craftsmen (an almost exclusively Jewish endeavor), and brokers. Some engaged in agriculture and some in money lending, though it was not the norm. Never a rich community, many Jews lived a marginal economic existence. However, there were usually more Jewish doctors in Marseille than Christian ones. We know from the chronicles of Benjamin of Tudela that among the Marseille Jews were a number of Torah scholars, philosophers, and psalmists.

Not much is known about the community of the Middle Ages, but it is acknowledged that it was divided geographically—one community in the upper town and one in the lower. Each was under a different jurisdiction though eventually they both came under the aegis of the local bishop. By the fourteenth century, Jews were administering their own schools, synagogues, mikvaot, and charities. The Jews of the time were the beneficiaries of some surprisingly liberal policies that accommodated their differences as Jews. For example, Jews were permitted to have a Passover flour market within the Jewish quarter rather than in the regular market where local law decreed all flour was to be sold. There were laws requiring residents to sweep their own streets on Saturday, but Jews were permitted to do this on Friday.

In 1481, however, Provence became part of France. Three years later, many Jews fled for their lives after mobs rampaged through the Jewish quarter on a spree of murder and theft. Many others were held in Provence forcefully by the local government.

By 1491, driven out of Spain by the Inquisition, Spanish Jews began to arrive in Marseille on their way to Italy and Constantinople, only to be denied permission to reside by the local council. In 1500, the Jews were forced to leave Provence completely. Rather than leave their homes, many Jews chose to convert.

In 1670, Jewish merchants attempted to settle once again in Marseille. Despite their financial success, which enriched the town coffers, locals objected to Jews living and worshiping in their midst, and Jews were once again thrown out in 1682.

A new community sprang up in 1760, and it established a synagogue in 1768 and a cemetery in 1783. Internal differences resulted in a community split in 1790, but a reunited community of about three hundred established another synagogue and cemetery in 1804. From that time on the group grew and established schools, charities, and other communal institutions, including, of course, the synagogue, which is still in use.

The division of France into occupied and unoccupied zones during the Second World War put Marseille into the latter between 1940 and 1942. As a result, many Jews fled there for refuge. But once the Germans occupied all of France, Jews of Marseille were mercilessly hunted down and deported to their deaths. As in other areas of German occupation, the synagogue was badly damaged and Torahs and siddurim (prayer books) were burnt.

After the war the amalgam of Jews from communities all over Europe and the Mediterranean who were in the city set about rebuilding the community and the synagogue. Jewish immigrants from North Africa augmented the population in the early 1960s, and it continues to thrive today as France's second largest Jewish community. Today there are dozens of synagogues, schools, cultural organizations, fraternal organizations, bakeries, butcher shops, restaurants, and other hallmarks of a vibrant community.

SIGHTS

Synagogue

The Grand Synagogue of Marseille. 117, rue de Breteuil. Tel: 04-91-37-49-64.

This was constructed in 1864 and today also contains the offices of the Consistoire de Marseille and other Jewish organizations. The interior is typical of synagogues constructed under the aegis of the Consistoire in the middle to late nineteenth century. Those familiar with synagogue interior construction will notice immediately the similarities between this and churches of the

Courtyard of the Grand Synagogue of Marseille

same period (i.e., the raised pulpits). As discussed in the first chapter on the history of the Jews in France, this construction was deliberate and was designed to make Judaism's outward trappings more consistent with those of Christianity. This is an Orthodox synagogue, and women sit in a gallery above to conform to Jewish law and tradition.

Nîmes

*A*S IN THE REST of France, Jews have come and gone from Nîmes for centuries—probably as far back as the seventh century. The earliest evidence of an established community dates from the tenth century, when Nîmes had a synagogue. Indeed, beginning in the eleventh century, one of the hills within the city walls was called Poium Judaicum and was the site of the Jewish cemetery (today Mont Duplan).

Mairie de Marseille

État Nominatif des Israelites qui ont fait leurs Déclarations au Bureau de l'État Civil de cette Mairie, en Conformité du Décret Impérial du 20 Juillet 1808

Noms et prénoms des individus	Date de la Déclaration
Bassano, Samuel,	6. Octobre 1808.
L'empronti, aimé	6.
Haros, abraham	6.
Barsulay, Rebecca, Épouse de abraham haros	6.
Haros, Joseph, fils de abraham	6.
Isaac, Louis.	7.
Dangioli, ange	7.
Dangioli, aimé fils de ange	7.
Ruelos, Marcus Moyse	10.
Louis, Rosa, Épouse Ruelos	10
Ruelos, Leon, fils de Marcus Moyse	10
Digne, Léa, Épouse de Isaac Bedaride	10.
Bedaride, isaac	10.
Bedaride, Naphtalie, hain, fils de isaac	10
Bedaride, Benestruc, fils ... id	10
Bedaride, gad, Camille ... id	10
16	

Registry of Jews in Marseille, 1808

Constantini Maïr Nissim, fils de abraham	15 Novembre
Darmon, Mardochée Chaÿ	15
Darmon, david	15
Darmon, abraham	15
Darmon, Lune	15
Busnach, Michel	16
Aboulquier aaron	16
Dalmedico, Villaux	16
Gozlan, Jacob	16
Provenzal, Estelle, épouse Gozlan	16
Gozlan, auge, fils de Jacob	16
Gozlan, zaphire, fille — idem	16
Gozlan, Léon, fils — idem	16
Gozlan isaac, ... idem	16
Benzadon, abraham	16
Cavaillon, roussé	16
Lazard, adelaïde	16
Coste, isaac	16
De Cassin, Mardochée	17

458

Certifié Véritable par Moi Soussigné, adjoint du Maire de Marseille,
Remplissant En Vertu de Sa délégation, les Fonctions d'Officier de l'Etat Civil.
fait à Marseille, En l'hôtel de Ville, le 24 avril 1810 : —

Registry of Jews in Marseille, 1808

The local Jews enjoyed fairly good relations with the local bishop—so much so that he had some success in protecting them from the anti-Jewish edicts issued from the 1284 Church synod that sat in Nîmes. Unfortunately, though, the bishop's good offices were no match for the general expulsion order from France in 1306 and the Jews had to quit Nîmes. Their property, as elsewhere, was forfeited to the Crown.

Though settlements were attempted again after various expulsion orders were rescinded, the animosity of the local population caused the community to move over and over again. After the expulsion of 1394, the community ceased to exist until the seventeenth century.

The seventeenth-century community began as the result of merchants from Comtat Venaissin coming to Nîmes to trade. Though in the middle of the century the local authorities based in Toulouse did not want them there, they were finally granted limited trading rights at century's end. In the middle of the eighteenth century, some forty families were living in Nîmes under the leadership of Rabbi Elie Espir from Carpentras. Although the community was small, it flourished for a time, then declined in population, and then was revitalized by the North African immigration.

SIGHTS

Synagogue

40, rue Roussy. Tel: 04-66-29-51-81. Built in 1793, the synagogue also contains a mikvah and a matzo bakery.

Nice

ODAY'S JEWISH COMMUNITY OWES its existence to immigrants from North Africa, but like so many towns and cities of Provence, Nice has had a small group of Jewish residents on and off since the Middle Ages. Documents show that in the fifteenth century there was a synagogue and a cemetery here. There was a local Jewish language, too—Judéo Niçois, a mixture of Hebrew and the local dialect.

As in other places at that time, Jews were required to wear an identifying badge. They had to live under a mixture of regulations that protected them in some ways and discriminated against them in others: There were laws against forced baptism, but they had to live in a designated Jewish quarter. Commerce was restricted, but some professions such as medicine were completely open. Later, in the sixteenth century, constraints on money lending were lifted and Jews were free to practice one of the few means of commerce open to them.

In the mid-seventeenth century, after it became a free port, Nice received Jewish immigrants from Italy, the Netherlands, and Oran (Algeria). The new residents did not have to live in the Giudaria (ghetto, the present rue Benoît Brunice) and enjoyed a high degree of freedom, including freedom from some taxes. But in the early and mid-eighteenth century, new restrictions were enforced and Jews had to move back to the ghetto.

Between 1792 and 1814 Nice became part of France, and that union meant the new French emancipation for the Jews. But as had been happening for centuries, France's political turmoil translated into turmoil for the Jews, and they had to go back to the ghetto when France lost Nice to Sardinia in 1828. Emancipation would not come until 1848. By 1860, when Nice was once again French, Jews had begun to reap some of the benefits of civil rights.

On the eve of World War II, some five hundred Jews called

Nice home. As Nice was initially occupied by Italy and not Germany, the first years of the war were less harsh than they were for Jews in German-occupied France or in Vichy France. As a result, Nice became a place of refuge for Jews and many Jewish organizations. But once the German-Italian armistice was signed in 1943, Germany invaded Nice and began business as usual. Alois Brunner, the SS officer in charge of Jewish affairs, saw to it that some five hundred Jews were rounded up and shipped out within a period of five months. In addition, many Jews were murdered in Nice. It was only through the help of a largely compassionate local population and clergy that many Jews escaped the fate of their brethren. It was the survivors, along with immigrants from North Africa, who built today's thriving Jewish community in Nice. France's current chief rabbi, Joseph Sitruk, though born in Tunisia, grew up in Nice.

SIGHTS

Synagogue

Grande Synagogue. 7, rue Gustave-Deloye. Tel: 04-93-92-11-38. The synagogue's stained-glass windows are particularly lovely. They were designed by artist Theo Tobiasse.

Cemetery

Cimetière du Château contains graves going back to 1626.

Aix-en-Provence

NO TRACE REMAINS OF this community, which was established in the Middle Ages and was expelled a number of times. But not far from Aix there is a memorial at the Les Milles internment camp.

SIGHTS

Internment Camp

Les Milles. Tel: 04-91-04-75-00, or contact the Tourism Office at 04-42-26-02-93. Hours: Monday–Friday, 9 A.M. to 12 noon, 1 P.M. to 4 P.M. Railway car is open Monday, Wednesday, and Thursday, 9 A.M. to 12 noon, 2 P.M. to 6 P.M., and Tuesday and Friday, 9 A.M. to 12 noon.

To get to the camp take the number 15 bus from La Ronde, the large traffic circle in the center of Aix (which locals never refer to by its official name, place du Général de Gaulle), and tell the driver to let you off at the Camp des Milles. By car from La Ronde, follow the avenue des Belges to the first traffic circle and then take the avenue Pierre Brossolette that comes out of it. Follow it across the Pont de l'Arc and then take avenue Ernest Prados that veers off to your right after the bridge. Avenue Ernest Prados turns into the route des Milles. Follow the signs to the Camp des Milles.

At the tile works in Les Milles, a town near Aix-en-Provence, the French set up a camp for foreigners just after the outbreak of war in 1939. In it were housed mostly Jewish anti-Nazi refugees from Germany and Austria including Max Ernst, Hans Bellmer, and Max Lingner. Once France surrendered to the Germans in June 1940 it became an internment camp for Jews being shipped out of France. In August and September 1942, the French government at Vichy ordered some two thousand Jews from Les Milles to the camp at Drancy and then to Auschwitz. The camp was closed in 1943.

The camp lay in disrepair and anonymity for decades until the mid-1980s, when a project to make it a museum was started. Across the road and a few hundred yards from the museum is a replica of the kind of freight car used to transport prisoners.

Arles

SIGHTS

Museum

Lapidary museum: Arlaten Museum. 29, rue de la République. Hours: 9 A.M. to 12 noon and 2 P.M. to 6 P.M. Closed Mondays. Jewish ritual and historical objects from Provence. Make inquiries at the Tourism Office, Esplanade des Lices. Tel: 04-90-96-29-35.

Old Jewish Quarter

The present rue du Docteur Fanton was the medieval rue de la Juiverie. When the Jews were expelled from the region in 1495, the Jewish quarter was destroyed and incorporated into the rest of the city.

Provence Resources

AVIGNON

Synagogue: 2, place Jérusalem. Tel: 04-90-85-21-24.
> Daily morning and evening minyan; Shabbat minyan.

Mikvah: 7, rue des Sept-Baisers, Montfavet.
Tel: 04-90-86-30-30.
Kosher food: Inquire at the synagogue.

AIX-EN-PROVENCE

Synagogue: 3 bis, place Jérusalem.
Tel: 04-42-26-69-39.
> Daily morning and evening minyan; Shabbat and festival minyan.

Kosher grocery: 7, rue de Sévigné.
Tel: 04-42-59-93-94.

CARPENTRAS

Synagogue: place de la Maire. Tel: 04-90-63-39-97.
> Shabbat and festival minyan.

CAVAILLON

Information: The president of the local community is M. Maurice Benarousse. Tel: 04-90-71-74-85.

MARSEILLE

Synagogue: 117, rue de Breteuil. Tel: 04-91-37-49-64 or 04-91-81-13-57.

Daily morning and evening minyan; Shabbat and festival minyan.

Note: There are many synagogues in Marseille; the one above is the historic one. For others contact the chief rabbi's office. Tel: 04-91-71-18-38.

Mikvah: 47, rue St. Suffren. Tel: 04-91-81-45-15 or 04-91-53-20-56.

This is one mikvah of many.

Kosher Restaurants

Aux Délices d'Eden. Centre Commercial. Tel: 04-91-75-12-72.

Beth Din, dairy, Italian.

Chinatov. 63, rue Négresko. Tel: 04-91-22-16-02.

Beth Din, meat, Chinese. Dinner weekdays and Sunday lunch only.

Le Moriah. 215, rue du Rouet. Tel: 04-91-78-59-12.

Beth Din, meat.

Natanya. 17, rue du Village. Tel: 04-91-42-05-31.

> Beth Din, meat.

Pizza Breteuil. 133, rue de Breteuil. Tel: 04-91-37-20-20.

> Beth Din, dairy, Italian.

Kosher Pastry Shops

Avyel Cash. 25, rue St. Suffren. Tel: 04-91-57-17-78.

> Beth Din, Pareve.

Erets. 205, rue de Rome. Tel: 04-91-92-88-73.

> Beth Din.

Kosher Grocery

Bon Goût. 28, rue St. Suffren. Tel: 04-91-37-95-25.

Bookstores

Arche du Livre. 8, rue Mazagran.
Tel: 04-91-48-08-08.

Jaysber—Librairie Hébraïque. 95, rue Saint-Pierre. Tel:
04-91-48-08-80.

NÎMES

Synagogue and community center: 5, rue Angoulême.
Tel: 04-66-76-27-64.

> Daily morning minyan; Shabbat and festival minyan.

Mikvah: 40, rue Roussy. Tel: 04-66-64-20-13.

Kosher food: Community center, 5, rue Angoulême.
Tel: 04-66-76-27-64.

NICE

Synagogue: 7, rue G. Deloye. Tel: 04-93-85-82-06.

Daily morning and evening minyan; Shabbat and festival minyan.

Mikvah: 22, rue Michelet. Tel: 04-93-51-89-80.

Kosher Restaurants

Le Leviathan. 1, avenue Georges Clemenceau.
Tel: 04-93-87-22-64.

Beth Din, dairy, fish, pizza.

Le Richone. 26, rue Pertinax. Tel: 04-93-13-82-69.

French cuisine, tea salon, Shabbat meals.

Lechem Chamaim. 22, rue Rossini.
Tel: 04-93-88-47-01.

Beth Din, dairy, fish, wood-fire pizza.

Kosher Bakery and Pastry Shops

Au Pavé d'Argent—Cauvin. 10, rue Blacas.
Tel: 04-93-85-13-71.

Beth Din.

Maison Guez. 87, route de Laghet.
Tel: 04-93-54-93-90.

Beth Din.

Mickael. 37, rue Dabray. Tel: 04-93-88-81-23.

Beth Din de Nice.

Kosher Groceries

Espace Cacher. 25, avenue Auber.
Tel: 04-93-88-81-92.

Mickael. 37, rue Dabray. Tel: 04-93-88-81-23.

Riviera Cacher. 11, avenue Villermont.
Tel: 04-93-92-92-00.

Super Cash Colbo—Ouzana. 14, rue Michelet.
Tel: 04-93-52-15-15.

Note: Some of the large supermarkets in surrounding towns have kosher sections (Casino in Juan-les-Pins; Casino in Cannes; Casino and Champion in Antibes).

Bookstore

Librairie Judaica Tanya. 25, rue Pertinax.
Tel: 04-93-80-21-74.

CHAPTER TEN

The Alps

ACCORDING TO MOST DOCUMENTATION, Jews have lived in this area of France since the ninth century, when it was the former province of Dauphiné. In that era, they lived mostly in Vienne. From the beginning of the fourteenth century, there were Jewish communities in Grenoble, Briançon, Crémieu, Nyons, Serres, Valence, and Vizille.

Jews expelled from France in 1306 were welcomed in Dauphiné along with Jewish refugees from Comtat Venaissin in 1322. But the welcome on the one hand did not prevent instances of blood libel (1247) or accusations of complicity in the Black Death (1348).

When Dauphiné became part of France in 1349, the Jews of the region were permitted to retain the freedoms they had enjoyed under the previous administration, although restrictions were placed on them. But by 1390 Jewish taxes were so debilitating that many began to leave. Ever mindful of the financial advantages of having Jews living in his region, the local ruler attempted to prevent their departure, even going so far as to offer incentives for staying. But it was to no avail. So from roughly the beginning of the sixteenth century the region had no Jews at all.

Grenoble became the site of a small Jewish settlement at the beginning of the eighteenth century, but by 1717 its members had been expelled by an act of Parliament.

Grenoble

THE CAPITAL OF THE department of Isère and the former capital of Dauphiné, Grenoble has had a Jewish community on and off since the fourteenth century. Following the expulsion from France in 1306, some Jews were permitted to settle here by the ruler Humbert I. But in 1348, in the wake of the Black Death, nearly one hundred Jews were arrested, tried, and burned at the stake because they were believed to be responsible for the plague. There was no Jewish community in Grenoble again until 1717, when some refugees from Comtat Venaissin tried to settle there, only to be thrown out by the city fathers. The present community was formed after the French Revolution.

The Italians occupied Grenoble during World War II, followed by the Germans. Because of its mountainous location and its proximity to the borders of Switzerland and Italy, Grenoble served as a hiding place and a center of Jewish resistance.

In 1943, Isaac Schneerson, along with several Jewish organizations and scholars, secretly organized the Centre de Documentation Juive Contemporaine or CDJC (Contemporary Jewish Documentation Center) in order to collect and preserve Jewish documents. Acutely aware of the slaughter going on all around them and under pain of death, these courageous souls were able to document the activities of the Germans and their French collaborators.

After the liberation of France by the Allies in 1944, the CDJC was moved to Paris, and since 1956 it has been housed in a building on rue Geoffroy l'Asnier in the 4th arrondissement, along with the Memorial to the Unknown Jewish Martyr. (See the 4th Arrondissement section of chapter 2.)

As if the war and the Shoah were not enough, many Jewish families had to fight other battles. One such case was that of the Finaly family.

The Finaly Case

Fritz Finaly, a Viennese Jewish doctor, and his wife immigrated to France following the 1938 Austrian anschluss (unification) with Germany. They settled in Grenoble and had two sons— Robert in 1941 and Gerald the following year. Once France began to deport foreign-born Jews, the Finaly children were put in the care of a public school in Grenoble so that they would be safe. In 1944 Mr. and Mrs. Finaly were deported; like many, they never returned. Their children were turned over to Notre Dame de Sion, a Catholic missionary organization founded by David Drach, the converted son-in-law of Emanuel Deutz, one of France's first chief rabbis. Eventually the boys were put in the care of Antoinette Brun, the director of a Grenoble children's home. Brun wanted to keep the boys as her own and raise them as Catholics. After she was granted custody by the French government, she arranged for their conversion to Catholicism.

But three of Fritz Finaly's sisters survived the war and one of them traced her nephews to Antoinette Brun. The sisters were unaware of what had actually transpired because Brun lied to them and said the children were being raised as Jews.

Unable to wrest the boys from Brun, the sisters took the matter to court. During the five years that the case was in litigation, Robert and Gerald Finaly were moved from one Catholic institution to another. At one point they were hidden in a monastery and their whereabouts were unknown. But in 1953 France's highest court ordered the children's return to their family, and they went to live with their aunt in Israel.

Today, Grenoble's Jewish community is mostly North African in origin.

SIGHTS

Museum

Museum of the Resistance. 14, rue Hébert. Tel: 04-76-42-38-53. Hours: 9 A.M. to 12 noon, 2 P.M. to 6 P.M. Closed Tuesdays and December 25, January 1, and May 1.

The museum chronicles life in the Isère during the German occupation. As in most French museums of this kind, you have to look hard to find evidence of French collaboration with the occupiers.

Lanslevillard

*H*IGH IN THE FRENCH Alps, in this little town's Chapel of Saint Jean de Maurienne, is a mural that depicts Jews sitting around the figure of the Church and learning her "truths."⁹

CHAPTER ELEVEN

Lyon and Auvergne

*J*EWS HAVE LIVED IN THIS region since at least the fifth century. By the middle of the thirteenth century, there were communities in the towns and cities of Auzon, Bourges, Clermont-Ferrand, Ennezat, Langeac, Monton, Oilac, Peissin, Pont-du-Château, Puy-Roger, Ris, Rochefort, Taleine, Veyre, and Vichy. They left, along with the Jews of other parts of France, following the general expulsion order of 1306. They returned to the towns of Ennezat, Lignat, and Montaigut-en-Combraille in 1359 and stayed for a few decades, until the expulsion from France in 1394.

Bourges

*E*VIDENCE OF EARLY JEWISH life in Bourges is sketchy, but a few documents tell us that there was some sort of Jewish community during the fifth and sixth centuries. We know from those same documents that much effort was expended trying to convert local Jews. Those who would not convert were thrown out. But some of those who did convert to Christianity assumed high positions in the Church and ended up persecuting other Jews.

There is no community to speak of today—it died out after the expulsions of the fourteenth century—but the building at 79, rue des Juifs, near the cathedral, is believed to have been an eleventh-century synagogue. During World War II, hundreds of Jews found temporary refuge in Bourges.

SIGHTS

Cathedral

Cathédrale St.-Etienne. Place E. Dolet. In the Chapel of Notre Dame de Lourdes is a representation of the relationship between Judaism and Christianity similar to that depicted in windows in the Rouen cathedral. According to this version, the Torah (the first five books of Moses and part of what Christians refer to as the Old Testament) is a foretelling of the events of the Christian version of the Bible (the New Testament). The windows portray scenes that foretell the rise and triumph of the Christian church and the downfall of Judaism. The figures are similar to the Ecclesia and Synagoga statues in many French cathedrals. Here, both female figures are on opposite sides of the crucified Jesus. Synagoga's crown tilts on her head, she is blindfolded, her staff is broken, her head is bowed in defeat, and a moon in eclipse is over her head. A shining sun crowns the figure representing the Church. Here Judas represents Judaism and wears the pointed hat worn by medieval Jews.

Chalon-sur-Saône

*I*N THE NINTH CENTURY, the earliest days of the community of Chalon-sur-Saône, records indicate that many Jews were forced by Agobard, the archbishop of Lyon, to convert their children to Christianity. Agobard, who was very active in his anti-Jewish activities, also led attempts to boycott Jewish-made wine and meat.

Agobard's anti-Jewish writings are some of the earliest in French history. They include:

- *Epistula de baptizandis Hebraeis* ("On the Baptism [of the children] of Jews")
- *De baptismo judaicorum mancipiorum* ("On the Baptism of Jewish-owned Slaves")
- *Contra praeceptum impium de baptismo judaicorum mancipiorum* ("Against an Impious Precept Concerning the Baptism of Jewish-owned Slaves")
- *De insolentia Judaeorum* ("On the Insolence of the Jews")
- *De judaicis superstitionibus* ("On the Superstitions of the Jews")
- *De eavendo convictu et societate judaica* ("On the Necessity of Avoiding Association with Jews")[10]

In the Middle Ages, the grande rue (main street) was known as the Vicus Judaeorum (Jews' street). Here the Jewish community had many of the facilities they needed to live, including a mikvah and a matzo bakery. The area around the present rue des Places was a Jewish cemetery; in 1957 tombstones from the Middle Ages were uncovered. In the early medieval period, viticulture was an almost exclusively Jewish occupation, and the local Jews owned and cultivated many of the vineyards in the region. In addition, local Jews were engaged in making loans. In 1306, the year of the mass expulsion from France, that all changed.

Some Jewish families were allowed back in 1384, but they were expelled again in 1394. Another community was established in 1871, but today there are only a few families living here.

SIGHTS

Cemetery

A cemetery dating back a few hundred years can be found on rue St.-Jean des Vignes. Visits can be arranged by calling the local Jewish council members, M. Joseph Assayag, M. Michel Oiknine, or M. Frédéric Levy, at 03-85-80-94-50.

Clermont-Ferrand

CLERMONT-FERRAND HAS THE distinction of providing us with the oldest written records (470 C.E.) of Jewish presence in France—the letters of Sidonius Apollinaris, the town bishop. Local Jews were on good terms with the bishops until the late sixth century, when Bishop Avitus began a program of forced conversion. More than five hundred Jews were baptized and the rest escaped to Marseille. A synagogue was destroyed in 576.

A new community took root in the tenth century, and vestiges of that time are evoked in the names Fontgieve (Jewish Fountain), Montjuzet (Jewish Mountain), and rue du Faubourg-des-Juifs. But after this period, Jews did not live in Clermont-Ferrand again until the end of the eighteenth century, and there was no formal community until the beginning of the nineteenth century.

During the German occupation and the war, Clermont-Ferrand was in unoccupied France—that is to say, it was controlled by the Vichy regime. For a time, it was considered a relatively safe haven. The number of Jewish refugees reached eighty-five hundred at one point, but beginning in the summer of 1942 they were forced to leave.

SIGHTS

Synagogue

20, rue des 4 Quatre Passeports. The nineteenth-century building, whose interior is not well maintained, can be visited by calling the community center at 03-73-93-36-59.

Cemetery

Not far from Clermont-Ferrand, in the town of Ennezat, is a medieval Jewish cemetery. Information on visits may be obtained by calling the community center at 03-73-93-36-59.

Lyon

NOT MUCH IS KNOWN about the Jewish population that historians believe lived in Lyon in the second century. But a story among the Jews of the Middle Ages tells of boatloads of Jews captured in the fall of Jerusalem (70 C.E.) landing in Lyon.

More substantial documentation begins in the ninth century, when Lyon was home to a large, well-to-do community with some degree of political power. Here, as in other areas of France at the time, Jews were engaged in agriculture and viticulture. Their products were sold to Christians as well as Jews and also to the various royal households. As was the custom of wealthy people of their day, Jews owned slaves. They were also able to employ Christians in their commercial enterprises. That alone is indicative of good relations with their Christian neighbors and with the Church authorities. In addition, Jews also held public service positions as tax collectors.

During this period, Jews lived in the rue de la Juiverie at the foot of Fourvière hill. Here, as in other areas, friction between Jews and Christians often began as a theological problem. In Lyon, some Christians attended Jewish religious services. Indeed, many preferred them to their own. But this was anathema to Bishop Agobard, who hoped to preach Christianity to Jews and convert them. In 820, his attempts to forcibly convert Jewish children were met with strong opposition not only from their parents, but also from the emperor Louis the Pious. The bishop was stubborn and Louis had to persuade him of the error of his ways on several occasions by sending special ministers of Jewish affairs. Agobard remained undaunted, as did his successor, Amolon.

Lyon was not part of the French kingdom, so its Jews were not subject to the many and routine expulsion orders from France. Nonetheless, in 1250 they were expelled from Lyon and there was no organized community again until the fourteenth century, though there were some Jews in residence in the thirteenth century.

In the sixteenth century, groups of Jews came to settle and were soon forced to leave. In 1775, several families from Comtat Venaissin, Alsace, and Bordeaux applied for the right to open a cemetery, but it wasn't until 1795 that permission was granted and a cemetery was established at La Guillotière.

The small community, which was not wealthy and lived in poor conditions in the rue de la Barre and the rue Lanterne, was augmented by an immigration from Alsace and Lorraine in 1830. By 1840 the population had risen to seven hundred, and then to twelve hundred by 1854, at which point they had a salaried rabbi and formed a consistoire of their own. The synagogue on the quai Tilsitt, which is still in use, was opened in 1864.

Under the terms of the armistice with Germany in June 1940, Lyon was a so-called free city. A number of Jewish organizations from occupied France made their headquarters here, including the Consistoire Central. As a result, all Jewish life in France was centralized in Lyon during the occupation and the war, and the city was able to provide a refuge for a significant number of Jews. Because it was also headquarters for the Jewish resistance, which operated apart from the French Resistance, many of its leaders were arrested here. There was occasional cooperation between the two groups, and Lyon probably had one of the strongest resistance movements in all of France due in large part to the Catholic cardinal Gerlier. But it was here that German brutality against the Resistance was also strongest.

Lyon became home to many Jewish refugees at war's end, and with the influx of Jews from North Africa in the 1960s, today's greater Lyon community numbers some thirty-five thousand.

Klaus Barbie

In November 1942, SS Hauptsturmfuehrer (captain) Klaus Barbie, who would become known as the Butcher of Lyon, was named chief of the Lyon Gestapo, a position he would hold for two years. Barbie was responsible for the torture and death of many leaders of the French Resistance, including Jean Moulin, Charles de Gaulle's representative. As if that were not enough, over four hundred Jews were deported on his orders. He was not above carrying out murder himself and is known to have shot any number of people during his tenure in the Lyon Gestapo.

But Barbie, unlike his victims, was a survivor, and he landed a job with the U.S. army counterintelligence corps in Germany after the war. French attempts to extradite him were futile, as he was an indispensable spy. Eventually he escaped to

Bolivia in 1951, where he lived under the name Klaus Altmann. Tried in absentia in France and sentenced to death, Barbie nonetheless managed to evade justice. In 1971 French Nazi hunters Serge and Beate Klarsfeld located him. But it wasn't until 1983, following repeated appeals by the French, that he was expelled from Bolivia and brought to France for trial. In July 1987, following a two-month trial at which he refused to be present for much of the time, he was found guilty and sentenced to life in prison—the maximum penalty under French law. He died in 1991.

The trial received worldwide attention and was the topic of the day in France. Ambivalent feelings on the part of the French, along with actual opposition to the trial, made it the subject of discussion in and out of the mass media. Jews feared outbreaks of anti-Semitism; the French worried about once again raising the issue of collaboration with the Germans; and Holocaust deniers used it to trot out their whimsical version of history.

SIGHTS

Old Jewish Quarter

Just behind the Church of St. Paul is a remnant of an old Jewish quarter, which contained a synagogue, a cemetery, and other community institutions, although nothing but the street name remains.

Synagogue

13, quai Tilsitt. Built in 1864. Located on the left bank of the Saône River, facing the Church of St. George, this is an official French historic monument.

Sephardic Synagogue

47, rue Montesquieu. Built in 1919.

Cemetery

La Mouche Cemetery. 11, rue Abraham Bloch, 7th. Built in 1790. Buried here are Resistance leaders murdered during World War II. The street is named for the chief rabbi of Lyon who died at Taintrux in 1914.

Museum

Musée St.-Pierre. Centre d'Histoire de la Résistance et de la Déportation. 14, avenue Berthelot, 7th. Hours vary; call 04-78-72-23-11 for visiting information. A medieval Jewish tombstone is on exhibit.

Monument

Monument to victims of Nazi barbarism. Place Bellecour, 2nd.

Izieu

Musée Mémorial des Enfants d'Izieu. Tel: 04-79-87-20-08 or 04-79-87-20-00. About forty-five miles east of Lyon is the village of Izieu. On April 6, 1944, Klaus Barbie's henchmen arrested forty-one children and five women who were in hiding. They were sent to Auschwitz in August.

Lyon and Auvergne Resources

*L*YON HAS MANY KOSHER restaurants, takeout stores, bakeries, grocery stores, and other food shops in addition to the ones listed. It also has numerous synagogues (mostly Orthodox). For information, call the Consistoire at 04-78-37-13-43. In addition, three publications, *La Voix Sépharade, Le Bulletin du Consistoire,* and *Harpchaar,* will have listings. Many Jews also live in the suburb of Villeurbanne, and you will find numerous synagogues and kosher places there, too.

SYNAGOGUES

Grande Synagogue. 13, quai Tilsitt.
Tel: 04-78-37-13-43.

Communauté Juive Libérale. 18, rue du Bât d'Argent.
Tel: 04-78-00-27-13.

Synagogue Sépharade. 317, rue Duguesclin.
Tel: 04-78-58-18-74.

Daily and Shabbat minyan.

MIKVAOT

Mikvé Chaare Tsedek. 18, rue St.-Mathieu.
Tel: 04-78-00-72-50 or 04-78-75-52-93.

Mikvé Neveh Chalom. 317, rue Duguesclin.
Tel: 04-78-58-18-74.

Mikvé Rav Hida. 501, avenue de la Sauvegarde.
Tel: 04-78-35-14-44 or 04-78-64-98-94.

KOSHER RESTAURANTS (BETH DIN)

Henry Lippmann. 4, rue Tony Tollet. Tel: 04-78-42-49-82.
Meat.

Le Grillon d'Or. 20, rue Terme. Tel: 04-78-27-33-09.
Meat.

KOSHER TAKEOUT (BETH DIN)

Château Perrache. 12, cours Verdun. Tel: 04-72-77-15-00.
Henry Lippmann. 4, rue Tony Tollet. Tel: 04-78-42-49-82.
Ittah. 267, avenue Berthelot. Tel: 04-78-00-82-35.
Le Grillon d'Or. 20, rue Terme. Tel: 04-78-27-33-09.

KOSHER BAKERY

Jo Délice. 44, rue Rachais. Tel: 04-78-69-22-98.

KOSHER GROCERY

Cacher Villeroy. 32, rue Villeroy. Tel: 04-78-71-72-22.

BOOKSTORE

Decitre. Place Bellecour. Tel: 04-72-40-54-54.

CHAPTER TWELVE

Burgundy

*L*IKE JEWS IN OTHER PARTS of France, the early Burgundian Jews were involved in viticulture—especially in the towns of Chalon-sur-Saône and Mâcon—beginning in the tenth century. In addition, there were Jewish communities in the towns of Auxerre, Auxonne, Avallon, Baigneux-les-Juifs, Beaune, Bourg, and Dijon.

Jews in Burgundy labored under burdensome taxes over and above those paid by the rest of the populace. And although they enjoyed some protection in the sense that they were allowed to live in the region, they were nonetheless expelled with the rest of the Jews of France in 1306, and their property was seized. From 1311 to 1315, some returned to the same towns. The local duke, Philip the Bold, permitted twelve Jewish families to live under his domain in 1374 and then increased the number to twenty in 1380, and to fifty-two in 1384. In 1394 they were all expelled again.

Dijon

THE COMMUNITY HERE GOES back to the end of the twelfth century, when the Jews lived and had a synagogue on rue de la Petite Juiverie (now rue Piron), rue de la Grande-Juiverie (now rue Charrue), and the rue des Juifs (now rue Buffon). The cemetery was located on what is now rue Berlier, but it was destroyed after the 1306 expulsion.

Following the French Revolution, the community grew when some Jews from Alsace came to settle. The synagogue (on the rue de la Synagogue) was dedicated in 1879 and the cemetery dates from one hundred years before that.

During World War II, the Germans used the synagogue as a warehouse, and many of Dijon's Jews were deported and murdered in Auschwitz. Today's community is a strong one and is mostly of North African origin.

SIGHTS

Museum

Musée Archéologique de Dijon. 5, rue du Docteur-Maret. Hours: 9 A.M. to 12 noon, 2 P.M. to 6 P.M. Closed Tuesdays.

The museum holds an important collection of twelfth- and thirteenth-century Jewish tombstones and tombstone fragments.

Synagogue

5, rue de la Synagogue. Tel: 03-80-66-46-47.

Dedicated in 1879. During the occupation, the Germans used the synagogue as a warehouse, as mentioned above. Though the lovely nineteenth-century edifice was spared from destruction during the war, the original pews did not survive. Those attending services sat on plain wooden benches until the synagogue was restored.

Mâcon

OCUMENTS DETAILING THE CHURCH'S mission-ary activity in the ninth century note a Jewish community here at the time.

Jews in Mâcon owned fields and vineyards and lived in a quarter called Bourgneuf. There was a Jewish cemetery near Pontjeu—formerly known as Pont des Juifs (Jews' bridge). By the late fourteenth century only a handful of Jews still lived here, and there were only about fifty by the beginning of the Second World War. The community today remains small and is of North African origin.

SIGHTS

Museum

Musée des Ursulines. 5, rue des Ursulines. Tel: 03-85-39-90-38. Several tombstones that were excavated from the medieval Jewish cemetery near Pontjeu can be seen here.

Beaune

SIGHTS

Museum

Musée des Beaux Arts. Rue de l'Hôtel-de-Ville. Tel: 03-80-24-56-92. In this museum is an Ecclesia and Synagoga painting. In this sixteenth-century piece a hand is extended from the beam of the living cross. It is striking Synagoga, who has a scorpion on her shield. As is typical, Synagoga's eyes are blindfolded.[11]

Burgundy Resources

MÂCON

Synagogue: 32, rue des Minimes.

Friday night minyan.

DIJON

Synagogue: 5, rue de la Synagogue. Tel: 03-80-66-46-47.

Monday and Thursday minyan; Shabbat and festival minyan.

Mikvah: 5, rue de la Synagogue. Tel: 03-80-67-50-98.

Kosher grocery/butcher shop: Levy. 25, rue de la Manutention. Tel: 03-80-30-14-42.

CHAPTER THIRTEEN

Franche-Comté

THE JEWISH POPULATION of Franche-Comté has always been sparse. Historians can infer Jewish settlement in this formerly independent region dating from the 1182 expulsion from France. Documents from 1220 indicate the presence of a Jewish quarter in the town of Lons-le-Saunier. Two hundred years or so later there were small communities in Baume-les-Dames, Besançon, Lons-le-Saunier, and Vesoul.

Though Jews were welcomed because the high taxes they paid enriched the coffers of the local lords, many towns did not permit Jews to reside in them. As in many other places, their primary occupation was money lending.

In 1348 during the Black Death, when Jews all over Europe were blamed and persecuted for the deadly disease ravaging the continent, the Jews of Franche-Comté were arrested, imprisoned, and tortured, and their property was seized. The regent, Jeanne de Boulogne, banished all Jews. There was a brief respite from the banishment between 1384 and 1394, when, after Franche-Comté was reunited with Burgundy, some Jewish families were permitted to settle. Between 1409 and the Revolution, there were no Jews in Franche-Comté.

Besançon

THIS CITY, ANNEXED TO France in 1674, has a small Jewish community dating back to the middle of the thirteenth century, when Jews lived on what is now the rue de Richebourg. By the fifteenth century, Jews had left the city, and the government sold the land where the cemetery stood (near the present Porte de Charmont). Until the French Revolution, only the odd Jewish merchant could be found residing here.

In 1807, a new community of about twenty families settled in Besançon—under the auspices of the Consistoire de Nancy. Some Jews who left Alsace and Lorraine after the end of the Franco-Prussian War in 1871 settled here. The community was destroyed by the Germans during the occupation. Today's community numbers under two hundred families.

SIGHTS

Synagogue

23, quai de Strasbourg. Tel: 03-81-80-82-82. Moorish in style, this synagogue was built in 1865. Services on Shabbat and festivals.

CHAPTER FOURTEEN

Alsace-Lorraine

THE RICH JEWISH HERITAGE you will find here is unlike any in France. Nowhere else can you see the sheer number of eighteenth- and nineteenth-century synagogues spread out over such a distance. And nowhere else will you find a Jewish community with such a rural history.

As you tour this region, the forces of history will hit you right in the face. The language is French, but the architecture is German; the food and wine are German; many towns have German names; and often the street and town names are a hybrid—rue d'Unterlinden, for example, or the town of Bouxwiller, called Buchswiller when it was part of Germany.

Many sources mention Jewish communities in the Alsace towns and cities of Obernai, Mulhouse, Colmar, Molsheim, Sélestat, Haguenau, Guebwiller, Marmoutier, Rouffach, Ensisheim, Bouxwiller, Saverne, and Rosenheim as far back as the twelfth and thirteenth centuries. Benjamin of Tudela, the twelfth-century traveler who chronicled the Jewish world of his day, notes that there were Jews in Strasbourg around 1170. It is likely that some Jews expelled from France in 1306 went to Alsace, because after that period additional towns are documented as having Jews in historical records. The vestiges of many of those Jewish communities can be seen in the synagogues, cemeteries, and remnants of Jewish quarters, along with present-day communities.

Like Jews in other parts of France and the rest of Europe in the Middle Ages, the Jews of Alsace and Lorraine suffered through expulsions, blood libel accusations, and blame for the Black Death. They were driven out of cities and towns over and over again. Frequently they were only permitted to settle in the hamlets and villages surrounding larger cities. In Strasbourg, Jews were allowed into town during the day for business, but had to be out by sundown. There were a few bright spots over the centuries; in Colmar in the fourteenth century and in Mulhouse in the fifteenth, they did have some rights.

The Armleder

Identified by leather armbands, this roving group of medieval German killers wreaked havoc on the Jews of Alsace from 1336 to 1339—just prior to the Black Death. Led by a man who claimed to have been directed by an angel to kill Jews, the group found many allies for its cause among the Christian citizenry, clergy, and nobility, including King Ludwig of Bavaria and the bishop of Strasbourg. Some 120 towns were overrun and thousands of Jews killed and their property confiscated by the state. It was not until the Armleder began to prey on Christians that the bishop of Strasbourg put a stop to its activities.

Nearly indistinguishable in manner and custom from other Ashkenazim (the Jews of central and eastern Europe), Alsatian Jews did develop some individual characteristics as a community: a synagogue liturgy called minhag Elzos and a Judeo-Alsatian language akin to Yiddish. (Yiddish developed during the Middle Ages in northeastern France and along the Rhine River in Germany. From there it migrated to Poland and Russia, and because it took on elements of other languages, it became a Yiddish quite different from the one spoken in its place of origin.)

Life for Alsatian Jews was difficult. They were exploited by the Christian aristocracy and forced to pay high tolls and taxes in order to do business in places where they were not residents, to wear identity tags, and to get permission to marry. There was a Jewish oath and a prohibition against owning land or any building other than one's own residence. Children born out of wedlock were forcibly baptized.

The 1648 Peace of Westphalia, which ended the Thirty Years' War and with it the Holy Roman Empire, made Alsace and Lorraine part of France.

The Glatigny Ban

Jews had lived in the town of Boulay since the end of the four-teenth century during the reign of Charles IV, Duke of Lorraine. And although there is really nothing of Jewish historical interest to see in Boulay, there is a sad story to tell about the town.

In 1669, Raphael Levy, a young merchant from Boulay (some sources say he was a rabbi), was accused of the rape and ritual murder (blood libel) of a young girl from nearby Glatigny. Despite the fact that her body was found and it was determined that she was eaten by wolves, Levy was burnt at the stake in 1670 following a trial that none could call just.

In 1699 his name was cleared by the parliament in Nancy. But because of this calumny, the rabbinate at the time decreed that it was forbidden for any Jew to spend even one night in Glatigny. That ban is still observed to this day.[12]

Becoming part of France did not change daily life in Alsace and Lorraine very much, and the life of the Jew was unstable to say the least. Many were moneylenders to the peasantry—an occupation fraught with danger as it was usually a pretext for anti-Jewish riots.

Others were small-time merchants or peddlers. France also did not want more Jews to settle there, and the French government restricted migration of Jews from other parts of France to Alsace throughout the eighteenth century. So odious were conditions that they spawned a civil rights movement.

The emancipation of French Jewry just after the Revolution came about largely through the efforts of a group of Alsatian Jews, and one Herz Cerf Berr, in particular. A wealthy merchant from Strasbourg by way of its suburb Bischheim, Cerf Berr had some business ties to the French court. He was supported in his civil rights efforts by such non-Jews as Honoré-Gabriel Riqueti (Comte de Mirabeau); Robespierre, the French revolutionist; and Abbé Grégoire, a Roman Catholic priest. But though there was support for Jewish rights in some circles, it was not widespread. There was strenuous opposition in the Chamber of Deputies and it was especially strong among the members from Alsace and Lorraine who predicted that Jewish emancipation would result in riots. Opposition didn't wane even after the passage of the equal rights law on September 27, 1791; those same forces continued to oppose it and led the effort to repeal it.

The sentiments of Alsatians being what they were, Jews didn't make much effort to integrate. But their new freedom of movement brought many to Strasbourg—so many that Strasbourg went from a Jewish population of about one hundred before the Revolution to a population of more than one thousand just ten years later.

By the middle of the nineteenth century, though, Jews had become pretty well integrated into Alsatian society—the result of legal reforms, a cessation of forced-integration tactics, the establishment of the Consistoire, and the expansion of liberal thinking. They thought of themselves not only as Jews, but also as Frenchmen. Many had begun to move away from the small towns that they had lived in for centuries to large cities—even to Paris. As in other parts of France, Jews entered industry and other professions and became successful. Religious education was augmented by a secular one and provided entrée into the universities. As a result, Jews also distinguished themselves in the arts and belles lettres.

Nonetheless, as French as they had become outwardly, from a religious point of view they were Jews. Any movement toward the reform of traditional Judaism was greeted with hostility by the rabbinate. Such infamous rejections of Judaism by sons of prominent families—like David Drach, son-in-law of one of France's chief rabbis, Emmanuel Deutz, and the Ratisbonne brothers, sons of the president of the Consistoire of the Lower Rhine—did nothing to change the attitude. (See chapter 1.)

Alsace and Lorraine lie in the northeastern region of France— the area bordering Germany. And as a result, they have borne more than their share of Europe's wars and social upheaval. France's defeat in the Franco-Prussian War in 1871 returned all of Alsace (except for Belfort) and part of Lorraine to Germany. But by this time, Jews had become so thoroughly integrated into French society that most chose to move to places like Paris, Lyon, and Elbeuf rather than live under a German regime. The community that remained was augmented by immigration from Germany proper. Though they accepted the political situation as unchangeable, they were never fully comfortable with German rule and were relieved when France reclaimed the region after Germany was defeated in World War I.

Though loyalty to France was not something the Jews of Alsace and Lorraine questioned in themselves, it was an issue for French non-Jews—particularly those in politics and in right-wing circles. And it would become a factor a few years later in the Dreyfus Affair. (See chapter 1 for a discussion of the Dreyfus Affair.)

Separation of church and state took effect in France in 1905, but when Alsace and Lorraine were returned to France in 1918, the French government decided, for political reasons, to make concession to the Catholic Church. As a result, the salaries of

Consistoire officials in Alsace and Lorraine, along with those of officials of other religions, continued to be paid by the state.

When the Germans occupied France, including Alsace-Lorraine, beginning in June 1940, they implemented their anti-Jewish policies immediately. Jews were moved to the French interior, and synagogues and cemeteries were destroyed or desecrated. At war's end, the Jewish community of France had suffered terrible losses, but surviving Alsatian Jews returned to the region and settled primarily in large cities such as Strasbourg. The village communities largely fell to ruin.

The present Jewish population of Alsace is around twenty thousand, with the vast majority, seventeen thousand, living in Strasbourg. The Lorraine community numbers about six thousand, with some two-thirds of the Jewish population living in Metz and Nancy. Though the local population was given a boost in the early 1960s by the influx of Jews from Algeria, it is today the only community in France that is predominantly Ashkenazic, though to be sure it is much more diverse than it once was. It still has its own Consistoire, and though the community is large and cohesive and is served by a number of communal and philanthropic organizations, it is beset by the same problems faced by Jews all over the world: intermarriage and a move away from the traditional faith.

The Synagogues of Alsace

YOU WILL SEE LITTLE of the synagogues of the Middle Ages and almost nothing from the fourteenth through eighteenth centuries, when synagogue construction was forbidden. During that period, an upper floor of a private house would often be used for services. Most of the synagogues you see today are from the eighteenth and nineteenth centuries, when, following emancipation, nearly every town and village had one. Some 176 synagogues were built in Alsace between 1791 and 1914.

Many towns and cities of Alsace and Lorraine have synagogues and other Jewish sites that are not open to the public. Most of the functioning synagogues are in the larger cities. Synagogues in smaller communities may only hold occasional services, perhaps on Rosh Hashanah and Yom Kippur. Some are just closed, awaiting the disposition of the owner, the Consistoire. In some cases, buildings that were once synagogues have been sold and are now used for something else—including private homes. For the most part, this chapter mentions only those places open to visitors. One day a year, usually a Sunday in late summer, the Jewish communities and local tourism offices present a program of Open Doors. At that time, sights not normally open are, some with local guides to show you around. This is part of a Europewide program, coordinated in Strasbourg, in which some sixteen countries participated in 2001. For information on upcoming dates, contact ADT, Mme Catherine Lehmann, 9, rue du Dôme, 67061 Strasbourg. Tel: 03-88-15-45-88. Fax: 03-88-75-67-64.

The Cemeteries of Alsace

THERE ARE DOZENS OF old Jewish cemeteries in Alsace—some going back to the fourteenth and fifteenth centuries. Many are still used and this guide will point you to them, but some are difficult to get to and others are closed. If you are interested in a specific cemetery not listed in the guide (for example, if you want to find a family member who was buried in a specific place), contact either the Office of the Chief Rabbi in either Colmar (Tel: 03-89-41-38-29) or Strasbourg (Tel: 03-88-32-38-87) for information, or the Office of Tourism in Strasbourg (Tel: 03-88-15-45-88). There are three things to note: Many of the older headstones are severely weather-beaten and difficult, if not impossible, to read; most inscriptions on older stones are in Hebrew; and Jewish cemeteries are frequently located on hilly and rocky land—land that was not fit for other uses.

Seeing Alsace and Lorraine

*T*HE BEST WAY TO cover the most ground as you tour Alsace-Lorraine is by car using Strasbourg or Colmar as a base—Strasbourg for the northern part of the region and Colmar for the southern—but if you need to you can do it all from Strasbourg. Though the roads are quite good and well marked, a detailed map is essential (Michelin map number 242, the Michelin motoring atlas for France, is excellent, or one of the Blay-Foldex maps).

Strasbourg

*T*HE JEWISH COMMUNITY OF Strasbourg has retained its predominantly Ashkenazic character, unlike most communities in France. This vibrant community, inheritor of Alsace's rich Jewish history, made a comeback from the devastation of the German occupation and the Shoah and is an integral part of life in the city.

The Jewish community you see today dates back to the tenth century, though evidence from that time is sketchy. Solid evidence places a Jewish community here at the end of the twelfth century. Still more documentation is available from the thirteenth and fourteenth centuries, when the existence of a Jewish quarter, synagogue, and cemetery are mentioned in Strasbourg's town records. Jews from other parts of Alsace settled in Strasbourg, as did Jews from Germany. By 1306 the population had reached nearly three hundred. It is believed that several Christian residents of thirteenth-century Strasbourg with the surname Jude (Jew) were converts from Judaism.

In Strasbourg, as in many other places, money lending was the chief Jewish occupation. Some of their best customers were Christian religious organizations. The community of Strasbourg was also rather wealthy if the tax roles are any indication, but the community's wealth had a downside. The already negative relationship between Jews and Christians fostered by Jewish money lending served as a pretext for the vicious accusation that Jews had poisoned water wells to spread the Black Death.

Jews also found themselves pawns in battles for power within the city—battles that had nothing to do with them. Such was the case in the mid-fourteenth century when the town council was divided on a number of issues. Accusations of spreading the plague had been made against Jews in a number of towns. The municipal councillors refused to pass judgment until investigations from all the localities were complete—and they were inclined to believe the Jews innocent of the charges to begin with. But that council faction was greatly outnumbered by a group of craftsmen who took for granted Jewish culpability in the well poisoning. The craftsmen forced the mayor and two other council members out; a new council was elected and immediately condemned the Jews of Strasbourg to be burned at the stake. Two thousand Jews were murdered in this manner on February 14, 1348, one day after the council's decision. All their possessions were taken by the municipality, and a one-hundred-year ban on Jewish settlement was instituted.

By the summer of 1349, the Black Death had claimed thousands of lives in Strasbourg. Even the Jews who had converted the year before in order to escape the fate of their brethren could not escape the wrath of the townspeople this time. As usual, such animosity reached to the highest places. In September 1349, Emperor Charles IV issued a pardon to Strasbourg for what they did to the Jews. So deep was this hatred that for more than four hundred years—until the French Revolution—Strasbourg commemorated the alleged treachery of those Jews by the nightly blowing of a horn.

During a brief lull in the ban in 1369, a few Jewish families were able to reside in Strasbourg in exchange for a large sum of money. But they too were forced out in 1388, and the ban was extended from its original one hundred years to perpetuity. Most moved to towns nearby and continued to do business in Strasbourg upon payment of a high toll, though such business dealings were strongly discouraged by the town fathers. Jews coming in to do business were often searched at the gate and then required to be accompanied by an employee of the town. If a Jew needed to spend the night, he was restricted to specific inns and had to pay an extra fee.

Conditions became easier under French control in 1681. In years to come, a few Jews who had business relationships with the nobility and the army were given permission to live in Strasbourg despite the general prohibition. One of those for whom special arrangements were made was Herz Cerf Berr, who would figure so prominently in the struggle for Jewish civil rights. Strasbourg's representatives to the National Assembly unanimously opposed civil rights for Jews. Nonetheless, once they were granted, Jews began to move to Strasbourg and establish the community we see today. Early in the nineteenth century, Strasbourg Jewry founded synagogues, a vocational school, a home for the elderly, and a rabbinical seminary. On the eve of World War II there were nearly ten thousand Jews in Strasbourg—over two-thirds of them born in France. The Germans murdered about one thousand during the war.

In June 1940, following the French surrender to the Germans, Strasbourg's chief rabbi René Hirschler created a community in exile in the southwestern French town of Périgueux. Most of Strasbourg's Jews had already been evacuated to that general area at the beginning of the war in September 1939. Rabbi Hirschler and other Strasbourg rabbis were tireless in their efforts to minister to their now widely dispersed group. All of the Strasbourg community in exile gave of themselves in resistance and rescue work, including evacuation to Palestine and to neutral Switzerland. Hirschler and others, for their efforts, were captured by the Germans and murdered in Auschwitz.

The center of today's Jewish community is the massive Synagogue de la Paix (Synagogue of Peace) on the rue du Grand-Rabbin René-Hirschler. It replaced the 1848 synagogue on the same site that was destroyed by the Germans. The building also houses a community center, nursery school, kosher restaurant, and several of the city's Jewish organizations. In addition to the main services, which follow the Ashkenazic tradition, you can also attend a Sephardic minyan in the same building. Strasbourg is home to yeshivas, Jewish philanthropic and fraternal organizations, Jewish newspapers, and a Jewish radio program. The highly regarded University of Strasbourg even has a chair in Jewish studies.

Though the Jews of Strasbourg are well integrated into the community at large, Alsatian anti-Semitism is there, even if only in the background. Since the end of World War II, a number of organizations have been established to prevent the return of Jewish property seized by the Germans and their French collaborators during the occupation, and also to prevent the construction of synagogues on city-owned land.

Many of Strasbourg's Jews live in the area around the synagogue—a lovely and fashionable neighborhood with lots of park space. But even though it has a large Jewish population, you will not win any friends by calling this the Jewish quarter. The term *Jewish quarter* has negative connotations not only here, but also all over Europe—not surprising given European history. Such a term in the United States would not be a big deal, but here it is practically an insult.

There are some seventeen thousand Jews in Strasbourg and it is the only city in France where the Jewish community is mostly

Ashkenazic. Like any other modern Jewish community, it struggles with issues like intermarriage and declining Jewish observance.

SIGHTS

Synagogue

Synagogue de la Paix, Rue du Grand-Rabbin René-Hirschler. Next to the lovely Parc des Contades, this imposing structure was built in 1958 to replace the synagogue on the same spot that was destroyed by the Germans during the occupation. The interior is equally impressive—a circular sanctuary nestled beneath a star of David. The synagogue has several minyanim (minyans), both Ashkenazic and Sephardic. In addition to the synagogue, the building houses a community center, the community's administrative offices, a kosher restaurant, and a school.

Cathedral

Cathédrale Notre-Dame. Place de la Cathédrale. To the left of the portal as you face Strasbourg's Cathedral of Notre Dame are two statues, Ecclesia and Synagoga, circa 1230. The one on the left represents Christianity—a woman adorned with a crown and wearing a flowing gown. She holds a staff with a cross in one hand and a chalice in the other, and she grins in triumph over her enemy. The one on the right represents Judaism. Her garment is disheveled and clings tightly to her body. Her staff is broken and the tablets of the Law are about to slip from her hand. As is typical of Ecclesia and Synagoga, we do not see her face; her head is bowed and she is blindfolded because she cannot see the "truth" of Christianity.

Next to the cathedral is the Musée de l'Oeuvre Notre Dame. A chronicle of the arts in Strasbourg and the Upper Rhine from the eleventh through seventeenth centuries, the museum houses some Jewish tombstones from the twelfth through fourteenth centuries in the museum courtyard. They are originally from a cemetery at the place de la République. 3, place du Château, Tel: 03-88-52-50-00. Hours: Tuesday–Saturday, 10 A.M. to 12 noon; 1:30 P.M. to 6 P.M.; Sunday 10 A.M. to 5 P.M. Closed Mondays and New Year's Day, Good Friday, May 1, November 11, and Christmas.

The rue des Juifs (Jew street) is the heart of the old Jewish quarter and one of Strasbourg's oldest streets. Over sixteen hundred years old, it was the Roman east–west road. On the end of the street farthest from the cathedral, number 30, between rue des Pucelles and rue de la Faisan, was the site of the twelfth-century synagogue; the community's bakery was at number 17, the mikvah at the corner of rue des Charpentiers, the butcher shop at 22 rue des Charpentiers, and the cemetery at the place de la République.

Number 15 was constructed in 1290 and is the only remaining building from this period that was inhabited by a Jewish family. Beginning in 1587, this section of the rue des Juifs was known as Zum Judenbad (to the Jewish bath).

In the heart of the Jewish quarter, at 20 rue des Charpentiers, is a thirteenth-century mikvah. Discovered during excavations in the neighborhood, it is not yet completely restored and in a fragile state. It's only open to the public on Saturdays in July from 10 A.M. to 6 P.M. For information call the Strasbourg Tourism Office at 03-88-52-28-20.

The small room containing the bath is three square meters and is made of brick. The bath has a capacity of five hundred liters of water and is directly connected to the water table. The water table is much lower today than it was in the Middle Ages in this part of the city, and it is no longer visible from here. You can see traces of the stone steps that led into the bath. There is also a circular rainwater receptacle. The niches in the walls were used for candles.

Cemetery

Koenigshoffen. 29, rue de la Tour. Tel: 03-88-29-03-55.

Museum

Across the river is Musée Alsacien. 23, quai St. Nicholas. Tel: 03-88-35-55-36. Hours: Monday–Saturday, 10 A.M. to 12 noon, 1:30 P.M. to 6 P.M.; Sunday, 10 A.M. to 5 P.M. Closed Tuesdays and some public holidays. Guided tours available for groups. There are two rooms that exhibit Alsatian Jewish ritual objects. The History Society of the Israelites of Alsace and Lorraine began to donate these objects in 1907. In addition, furnishings from synagogues throughout the region have been put together to create a model shtiebel (prayer room).

Bischheim

JEWISH SETTLEMENT BEGAN IN Bischheim, which is three miles north of Strasbourg, after expulsion from Colmar in 1512. Bischheim was the home of Herz Cerf Berr, who figured so prominently in the movement to secure civil rights for Jews during and after the Revolution. Until the French Revolution, this was one of the most important Jewish communities in France.

Mikvah in Bischheim

SIGHTS

Mikvah

Cour de Boecklin. 17, rue Nationale. Tel: 03-88-81-49-47. This house once belonged to David Sintzheim, one of the three rabbis who made up France's first chief rabbinate. The steep, sixteenth-century restored hollow staircase leads to a restored mikvah. The room above, the David Sintzheim room, depicts Jewish life in Bischheim and has a permanent exhibit of Jewish ritual objects.

Haguenau

*T*HE JEWISH COMMUNITY HERE goes back to the thirteenth century, and is one of the oldest in Alsace. By the middle of the fourteenth century Jews had been wiped out in riots resulting from the Black Death. The synagogue stood on what is now the place de la République. The end of the century saw the reestablishment of a community with a synagogue at 8, rue du Sel.

The town became a haven for Jews in the early sixteenth century, when Joseph ben Gershom of Rosheim convinced the emperor to rescind the expulsion decree. There has been a community here ever since, albeit small. Some 148 Jews from Haguenau died during World War II.

SIGHTS

Synagogue

3, rue du Grand-Rabbin Joseph-Bloch. Tel: 03-88-73-38-30.

Built in 1821, this synagogue, like most in the region, was damaged by the Germans during World War II and later restored.

Cemetery

Rue de l'Ivraie. The cemetery was established in the sixteenth century, but the oldest tombstone is from 1654. For information on visits contact the community administrative offices at 03-88-93-95-38, or the local Office of Tourism: place de la Gare, Tel: 03-88-93-70-00, Fax: 03-88-93-69-89.

Museum

Musée Historique. 9, rue du Maréchal Foch. Tel: 03-88-93-79-22. Hours: June 14–September 21, daily 2 P.M. to 6 P.M.; September 22–June 13, Monday, Wednesday–Friday, 10 A.M. to 12 noon, 2 P.M. to 6 P.M., Saturday and Sunday, 3 P.M. to 5:30 P.M.

The town historical museum has a collection of Jewish art and ritual objects.

Soultz-sous-Forêts

SIGHTS

Matzo Bakery

Les spécialités Paul Heumann. 42a, rue de Lobsann. Tel: 03-88-80-40-61. Tours available, but book in advance.

Pfaffenhoffen

SIGHTS

Synagogue

Passage du Schneeberg, just behind the Romain parking lot. Tel: 03-88-07-80-05. Built in 1791, this nonworking synagogue was recently restored with funds from the World Monuments Federation. The very discreet façade shelters a synagogue and community center. The synagogue is on the top floor, and the ground floor contains the community room, matzo bakery, mikvah, and a room for a traveler. A synagogue this old is rare in Alsace; most were built in the nineteenth century.

Synagogue at Pfaffenhoffen

Bouxwiller

SIGHTS

Museum

Musée Judéo-Alsacien. Grande-rue. Tel: 03-88-70-97-17. Hours: May 15–September 15, Tuesday–Friday, 9 A.M. to 12 noon, 2 P.M. to 5 P.M., Sunday, 2 P.M. to 5 P.M. September 16–May 14, first Sunday of each month, 2 P.M. to 5 P.M.

This synagogue was slated for demolition, but it was rescued for the express purpose of creating a museum, and in 1999 the Musée Judéo-Alsacien opened after ten years of preparation.

Synagogue at Pfaffenhoffen

The museum contains a model synagogue typical of small-town Alsace and a permanent exhibit detailing rural Jewish life in Alsace through the centuries, including how holidays, weddings, and ritual circumcisions were celebrated. There is a fine collection of Jewish ritual objects, some unique to Alsatian Jewry. There is even a section on famous Alsatian Jews—among them, the Marx brothers, whose father came from Alsace; four-time Oscar-winning director William Wyler (*Ben-Hur, Funny Girl, Roman Holiday, Wuthering Heights*); and Alfred Dreyfus, who, along with Wyler, was born in Mulhouse.

Old Jewish Quarter

Rue des Juifs. Parallel to the grande-rue, behind the church.

Musée Judéo-Alsacien in Bouxwiller

Ettendorf

SIGHTS

Cemetery

For information and visits call the Office of Tourism in Strasbourg. Tel: 03-88-15-45-88. Near Bouxwiller, this cemetery on over nine acres of bare and windswept hillside has been receiving Jewish dead since the sixteenth century and continues to do so today. Some of the sandstone grave markers go back to 1566.

South and West of Strasbourg

Rothau/Natzweiler

SIGHTS

Concentration Camp

Natzweiler-Struthof concentration camp (located thirty-one miles south of Strasbourg near the town of Natzweiler). Address: Direction Interdépartementale des Anciens Combattants et Victimes de Guerre, Service de Strasbourg, Cité Administrative, 677084 Strasbourg. Tel: 03-88-76-78-99. Hours: March–June, daily, 10 A.M. to 12 noon, 2 P.M. to 5:30 P.M.; July–August, daily, 10 A.M. to 6 P.M.; September–December 24, daily, 10 A.M. to 12 noon, 2 P.M. to 5 P.M. Tickets sold up to half an hour before morning close and up to an hour before evening close. To get there by car, take the N420 southwest to Rothau. Once in Rothau make a left onto D130 and follow the signs to Le Struthof, about five miles from town. If you're traveling by train, the ride from Strasbourg to Rothau takes about an hour, but it is not certain that you will be able to get transportation from the Rothau station to the camp. This is a difficult place to get to; a car is best, but you might be able to find some organized tour by calling the Direction Interdépartementale des Anciens Combattants et Victimes de Guerre, Service de Strasbourg at 03-88-76-78-99.

Established in May 1941 and used until August 31, 1944, this labor camp was in a particularly harsh climate—cold even in summer—and located close to large quarries where many prisoners were forced to work. Some twenty-five thousand people spent their last days here. The camp was commanded by Hans Huettig, Egon Zill, and Josef Kramer (known as the Beast of Belsen—a reference

Jewish cemetery in Ettendorf

to the death camp at Bergen-Belsen); many thousands were executed here.

It was mainly used for political prisoners from France (including female members of the Resistance) and southwestern Germany. Inmates from this camp were given over to the Reich University in Strasbourg for so-called medical experiments involving infectious diseases. In August 1943, Josef Kramer brought in one hundred Jewish prisoners from Auschwitz (in Poland), gassed them, and gave their bodies to August Hirt at the Reich University for his skeleton collection.

What remains of this infamous camp is a cemetery, a barracks, the front gate, and some isolated buildings. There is also a large monument that was erected many years after the end of the war.

Marmoutier

SIGHTS

Museum

Musée des Arts et Traditions Populaires de Marmoutier. 6, rue du Général Leclerc. Information from the Office of Tourism, Tel: 03-88-71-46-84. Hours: May–October, Sundays and public holidays, 10 A.M. to 12 noon, 2 P.M. to 6 P.M. Group tours are given Monday–Saturday by prior arrangement with the Office of Tourism.

Housed in a former Jewish residence, this interesting museum exhibits not only some wonderful Jewish objects and a mikvah, but also general Alsatian artifacts.

Westhoffen

SIGHTS

Synagogue

Place de la Synagogue (behind the post office). No longer in use, this mid-nineteenth-century Roman-Byzantine-style synagogue has a beautiful limestone façade. Just to the right of the synagogue grounds (as you face the synagogue) is a now-private residence that was once a Jewish school. If you walk around town in the vicinity of the synagogue you may be able to pick out vestiges of the Jewish community—painted-over mezuzahs on doors, slots for mezuzahs, Jewish street names carved into the stone of buildings.

Wasselonne

SIGHTS

Matzo Bakery

Entreprises René Neymann. 46, rue du 23 Novembre. Tel: 03-88-87-03-57.

Proprietor Jean Claude Neymann is the fifth generation of his family to run this small matzo bakery where he not only bakes matzo for Passover, but also does a brisk business in specialty matzo (i.e., special diets, special flours). Tours available, but book in advance.

Rosenwiller

*T*HE JEWISH COMMUNITY HERE has always been small, but many communities in the region used its cemetery.

SIGHTS

Cemetery

Route de Grendelbruch; stay to the right going toward Molkirch. Established in the fifteenth century and not far from Obernai, this is now a registered French historical monument. Herz Cerf Berr, who died in 1794, is buried here. For visits inquire at the Office of Tourism in nearby Obernai, place Beffroi, Tel: 03-88-95-64-13, Fax: 03-88-49-90-84.

Obernai

JEWS FIRST CAME HERE to live in 1215. In the fourteenth century, they were accused of causing the Black
Death and sentenced to die at the stake. There were no Jews in
Obernai again until the fifteenth century. When Obernai came
under French authority in 1647, Jews returned in small numbers,
and by World War II there were a few hundred in residence.

It is pleasant to walk around this quaint old town. Here, as in
the rest of Alsace, the juxtaposition of German architecture with
the French language makes you aware of the forces of history that
have played such a pivotal role in the region.

SIGHTS

Synagogue

9, rue de Sélestat. The neo-Romanesque building was dedicated in 1876 and rededicated in 1948.

Old Jewish Quarter

Local experts believe that a doorway on the ruelle des Juifs
(Jews' lane) was the location of Obernai's medieval synagogue
(built in 1454). If you look very carefully you can see Hebrew letters around the doorway, but because of centuries of weathering,
they are difficult to read.

At 43, rue du Général Gouraud, at the back of the courtyard,
you can see a number of elements that attest to the Jewish presence here. This was a synagogue of about eight by ten meters that
could seat seventy men and forty-nine women. Above the arcade
is the Hebrew date 5456 (1696); the synagogue was located on

the first floor. Under the entryway is a plaque engraved with two hands—the symbol of the kohanim—and the inscription RABBI SAMSON, THE KOHEN. On the side of the doorway is a slot for a mezuzah. Along the wall, especially at the staircase to your right, you can see decorative engravings of the aron kodesh (ark), which holds the Torah scrolls. This sort of décor is rare in Alsatian synagogues.

Additional information from the Office of Tourism, place Beffroi, Tel: 03-88-95-64-13, Fax: 03-88-49-90-84.

Goxwiller

SIGHTS

Winery

Raymond Koenig winery. 35, rue Principale. Tel: 03-88-95-51-93. Learn how kosher wine is made. Book in advance. Tours are free; there is a charge for tasting.

Benfeld

THIS ALWAYS-TINY COMMUNITY HAS a synagogue that was built in 1845 and is the only one in Alsace that escaped World War II with little damage.

SIGHTS

Synagogue

Rue de la Dime. Built in 1845 in the Florentine style.

Cemetery

The cemetery here goes back to the fourteenth century. For information on visits to the synagogue and the cemetery contact the Office of Tourism in Strasbourg, Tel: 03-88-15-45-88.

Colmar

*P*ART OF GERMANY UNTIL 1681, the Jewish community here probably goes back to the mid-thirteenth century. That medieval community, which owned a synagogue, mikvah, and cemetery, was located between the present rue Chauffour and the rue Berthe-Molly (then the rue des Juifs).

During the fourteenth century, the Black Death spread across Europe and killed millions. Though we know today that the bubonic plague is caused by bacteria and spread by rats and fleas, back then its transmission was often attributed to Jews. In Colmar in 1349, many Jews were burned at the stake outside town at a place called the Judenloch; those who escaped execution were thrown out of town. Twenty-nine Jewish families were permitted to come back in 1385, but by 1468 only two families were living within the town. In 1512, the remaining Jews were expelled again and forbidden to enter or trade in Colmar. As late as the eighteenth century, Jewish residence in town was restricted to just a handful.

Jews were once again permitted in Colmar after the French

Revolution. In 1808 it became the headquarters of the Consistoire of the Upper Rhine and in 1823 it became the seat of the Upper Rhine's chief rabbinate.

As it did to other towns and cities in France, the Second World War brought death and destruction to the Jews of Colmar. The synagogue, completed in 1842, was vandalized by the Germans, but it was restored in the 1950s by the present community.

As you walk around Colmar, particularly near the old Jewish quarter (the present rue Berthe-Molly, formerly the rue des Juifs), you will notice a number of stars of David on the tops of buildings. According to local experts and historians, these do not indicate former Jewish buildings, but former breweries. The medieval brewers guild used the symbol, and it may or may not have anything to do with Jews. But it is true that the star of David was not widely used as a Jewish symbol until the nineteenth and twentieth centuries. The typical Jewish symbol of old was a seven-branched candelabrum. But the coincidence of the stars of David within what was the Jewish quarter makes for some interesting speculation.

SIGHTS

Synagogue

3, rue de la Cigogne. Tel: 03-89-41-38-29.

Built in 1840, this synagogue was destroyed by the Germans during World War II and restored by the local community in 1959. Its neo-Romanesque style is typical of synagogue construction in France during that period.

Museum

Bartholdi Museum. 30, rue des Marchands. Tel: 03-89-41-90-60. Hours: 10 A.M. to 12 noon, 2 P.M. to 6 P.M. Closed Tuesdays.

The Katz Room within the museum houses a fine and intriguing collection of Jewish ritual objects, synagogue furnishings, and other items used by Jews in Alsace and Jews in general. The museum is located in the house of Frédéric Auguste Bartholdi, the sculptor of the Statue of Liberty.

Cemetery

Rue du Ladhof. Established at the beginning of the nineteenth century.

Church

Church of St.-Martin. A gargoyle known as la Truie aux Juifs (Jewish sow) is above this fourteenth-century church's eastern wall. It depicts a pig with a man's head wearing the hat worn by medieval Jews and feeding on the excrement of a lewd and devilish goatlike animal. This is a replica of a medieval piece.

Information

Colmar Tourism Office. 4, rue d'Unterlinden. Tel: 03-89-20-69-02. Fax: 03-89-41-34-13.

South of Colmar

Sigolsheim

SIGHTS

Winery

La Cave de Sigolsheim. 11, rue St.-Jacques. Tel: 03-89-78-10-10. Hours: Daily, 10 A.M. to 12 noon, 2 P.M. to 6 P.M.

Within this wine-producing cooperative not far from Colmar there is a kosher winery. Taste and purchase their wonderful Alsatian wines. Advance booking required for groups.

St. Louis/Hegenheim

*T*HIS WAS ONE OF the largest Jewish communities in Alsace at the end of the eighteenth century. But by the eve of World War II, only a handful of Jews remained. The early-nineteenth-century synagogue is now in private hands.

SIGHTS

Synagogue

Rue de la Synagogue. Built in 1907 and enlarged in 1933 to meet the demand of a growing community, this synagogue was badly damaged during World War II and later restored. Contact the Office of Tourism in St. Louis, Tel: 03-89-70-04-49.

Cemetery

Just outside the town of Hegenheim, route de Hagenthal; bear left; the cemetery is on the edge of town before you get to the forest. To see the cemetery, contact its treasurer, Tel: 03-89-67-27-87, or the Office of Tourism in St. Louis, Tel: 03-89-70-04-49.

Dating back to 1673, this cemetery near the Swiss border was used by many communities in the region, including some communities in Switzerland.

Lorraine

JEWISH SETTLEMENT HAS BEEN sparse in this former duchy, but it is believed to go all the way back to the fourth century. Some very small Jewish communities could be found during the Middle Ages up through the mid-fourteenth century. Here, as in other regions of France, the Jews went through periods when some few were permitted to settle and periods when they were expelled, as they were from Saint Dié on suspicion of sorcery. In the mid-fifteenth century, Jews were granted the right to live in places like Nancy, Lunéville, and Sarreguemines by Duke John II, but only twenty years later his successor, Duke René II, appropriated their property and threw them out.

By the sixteenth century, despite the laws prohibiting Jewish settlement, local nobility, ever mindful of the financial advantages of having Jews in their land, permitted some Jews to settle. But the position of the Jews involved in finance at the whim of the local lord was a precarious one, and one wrong move—even an innocent mistake—was enough to bring trouble to the entire community. Take the case of Samuel Levy, a rabbi and financier, who got involved in financial dealings with Duke Léopold of Lorraine, acting as his agent for the purchase of grain. The fiscal policies enacted when he was the duke's tax collector (1715–16) made him many enemies among the nobility, and he was driven from office and forced into bankruptcy. Following arrest and imprisonment, he was thrown out of Lorraine. He moved to Paris and died a pauper.

That situation was enough to turn Duke Léopold against Jews in general. Though at one time the duke had permitted Jewish financiers to settle in Lorraine, he now had no use for them. In 1720, he promulgated an edict that would place every Jewish activity under strict scrutiny. The following year, all Jews who had arrived in Lorraine after 1680 were expelled. Those remaining, some 180 families, were taxed heavily. In addition, they were restricted as to the appointment of rabbis and the establishment of synagogues and cemeteries.

Things eased up when Lorraine once again became part of France in 1766. On the eve of the French Revolution there were about five hundred families living in the region. The movement for Jewish civil rights was vigorously opposed in Lorraine, as it was in Alsace, and there were some in the province who demanded that Jews be expelled from France entirely—though there was hardly anything new about that suggestion.

Following Jewish emancipation and the division of the Lorraine community into the Consistoires of Metz and Nancy, life settled down and became far less precarious. The vast majority of Lorraine's Jews (nearly eleven thousand) lived in and around Nancy. By 1808 they began to establish synagogues, schools, and various community organizations. Following France's defeat in the Franco-Prussian War in 1871, Jewish refugees from Alsace (which had been taken by Germany) and the parts of Lorraine annexed by Germany moved to French Lorraine. The Treaty of Versailles (1919), which returned Alsace and Lorraine to France, resulted in an increase in the Jewish populations from immigration from eastern Europe. The Second World War took a great toll on Lorraine's Jews, and many died at the hands of the Germans.

Nancy

IN THIS CAPITAL OF the department of the Meurthe-et-Moselle, which was also the capital of the Duchy of Lorraine, the history of the Jews closely follows that of the region as a whole since this was always a place with the largest Jewish population. It was here that Samuel Levy became Duke Léopold's tax collector and here where Jews felt the brunt of the anti-Levy reaction.

Throughout much of the eighteenth century, Jews were forced to meet for prayer in makeshift accommodations. A formal synagogue was not built until 1788.

During the German occupation many Jews left Nancy or were deported. Many who fled to the relative safety of southern France were subsequently deported once the Germans took over in 1942. Very few survived the war. The city's seventy-two-year-old chief rabbi, Paul Haguenauer, refused to leave his congregation and met the same fate as the rest of them—some 744 people. Today there is a street named for him.

The community rebuilt itself after the war, and it thrives today with a full range of religious and communal institutions. The highly regarded University of Nancy, a magnet for students not only from France, but also from other countries, has a department of Hebrew studies.

SIGHTS

Synagogue

17, boulevard Joffre. Tel: 03-83-32-10-67. For visits during hours when services are not being held, contact Mr. Jacky Herrmann. Services are held daily and on Shabbat and holidays.

Built in 1788 and restored and enlarged in 1841, this is one of the oldest synagogues in both Alsace and Lorraine and is a French historical monument. During World War II, the Germans used it as a supply depot and were about to blow it up when American troops arrived to save it.

Museum

Musée Historique Lorrain. 64, grande rue (in the Duke's Palace), Tel: 03-83-32-18-74.

The Lorraine historical museum has a very important collection of Torahs, prayer books, and other Jewish objects.

Lunéville

*T*HE JEWISH COMMUNITY HERE was founded in 1753. In 1785 a synagogue, the first in France with the authorization of the Crown, was built.

SIGHTS

Synagogue

5, rue Castara. For visits contact Madame Françoise Job, Tel: 03-83-74-08-07.

Madame Job is a historian who has written extensively about Jewish history.

Verdun

*I*N THIS TOWN, WHICH figured so prominently in the horrific Word War I battle (June 1916), Jews have been in residence on and off since the ninth century. It was a main station on a slave trade route between England, Germany, and Spain, but Christian and Jewish sources differ on the participation of Jews in such commercial enterprises. Though Christian sources attribute the slave trade to Jews, material found in Jewish sources casts considerable doubt on this. Verdun was a center for Tosafists, notably the followers of Rabbenu Tam. (See chapter 1 for a discussion of the Tosafists.)

SIGHTS

Synagogue

Impasse des Jacobins. Contact Rabbi Daniel Dahan, Tel: 03-83-41-34-48.

Built in 1805 on the site of a Dominican monastery, this synagogue was destroyed during the Franco-Prussian War in October

1870. Reconstructed in 1872, its style is Moorish with tenth-, eleventh-, and twelfth-century Byzantine influences. The Germans gutted it and used it as a mess hall during the occupation, but afterward it was once again restored with the aid of Jewish members of the American army. Additional restoration to the façade was completed in 1996, after it was placed on the register of historic monuments in 1984.

Memorial

At Fort Douaumont, there is a memorial to French and foreign Jews who died for France during World War I. It was dedicated in June 1938 on the twenty-second anniversary of the Battle of Verdun.

Metz

IN THE MIDDLE AGES, the Vicus Judaeorum was Metz's Jewish quarter. But even earlier, in the ninth century, there were enough Jews here to warrant anti-Jewish edicts by the Church. In the late eleventh century, twenty-two Jews met their deaths at the hands of the zealots of the first crusade.

By the middle of the thirteenth century, not only were Jews forbidden to live in town, but any Jew who passed through had to pay a special fee. Stays were limited to three nights. This ban lasted until the middle of the sixteenth century, when the French took over and admitted three Jewish families—pawnbrokers.

The community grew little by little and numbered 120 on the eve of the seventeenth century. There was considerable anti-Jewish enmity during the trial of Raphael Levy, who was falsely accused of ritual murder and later executed. But under the protection of the French throne, though there were the usual restric-

Title page from a Chumash, the book of Vayikra
(Leviticus), published in Metz in the
eighteenth century

tions, some three thousand Jews called Metz home in 1748. Within the Jewish quarter they were even permitted to govern themselves. They had a synagogue, a cemetery, charitable institutions, free elementary education, and even a Hebrew press. The press, established by Moshe May in 1764, published Yiddish translations of books like Defoe's *Robinson Crusoe,* along with Talmudic and Jewish liturgical material. Several Hebrew printers followed May, and it was only with France's defeat in the Franco-Prussian War in 1871 that the work was terminated.

Of course, as with Jews all over France, the community of Metz was heavily taxed and encumbered by laws that restricted their economic activity. By the French Revolution they owed huge tax debts.

The movement for Jewish emancipation found its proponents in Metz's noted jurists Pierre Louis Lacretelle and Pierre Louis Roederer; and even the Marquis de Lafayette, hero of the American Revolution, was an advocate of Jewish civil rights. Metz was also the home of France's first state-sanctioned rabbinical seminary (Ecole Centrale Rabbinique), which was relocated to Paris in 1859.

Under the German occupation during World War II, the Jews of Metz, along with the rest of the Jews of the region, were brutalized, deported, and murdered. Some fifteen hundred Jews met this fate, including many of the community's rabbis. Synagogues and other Jewish institutions were desecrated. At war's end, the remnant of Jewry resolved to rebuild, and the results are evident today. The Consistoire of the department of the Moselle, which is located in Metz, encompasses some two dozen communities that in total are home to about eight thousand Jews.

SIGHTS

Synagogue

39, rue du Rabbin-Elie-Bloch. Tel: 03-87-75-04-44. French historic monument.

Alsace-Lorraine Resources

STRASBOURG

Synagogue

Synagogue and community center: 1A, avenue du Grand-Rabbin René-Hirschler. Tel: 03-88-14-46-50.

Orthodox. Daily morning and evening minyan; Shabbat minyan.

Mikvah: Tel: 03-88-14-46-68.

In the same building as the main synagogue and community center. Open weekday evenings.

Kosher Restaurants

Autre Part. 60, boulevard Clemenceau.
Tel: 03-88-37-10-02.

Beth Din, dairy, fish, pizza, tartes flambées.

Le Wilson. 25, boulevard Wilson. Tel: 03-88-52-06-66.

Beth Din, meat served at lunch. Dairy served at dinner except Tuesdays when meat is served. French cuisine, pizza.

Levy. 4, rue Strauss Durkheim. Tel: 03-88-35-68-21.

Beth Din, dairy, fish, salads, tartes flambées.

Kosher Grocery

Délices Cachères. 22, rue Finkmatt.
Tel: 03-88-36-71-01.

Kosher Takeout

Levy. 4, rue Strauss Durkheim. Tel: 03-88-35-68-21.

Grumbach—Le Carmi. 27, rue Sleidan.
Tel: 03-88-61-52-83.

King. 28, rue Sellenick. Tel: 03-88-52-17-71.

Le Wilson. 25, boulevard Wilson. Tel: 03-88-52-06-66.

Kosher Supermarket

Supermarché Match. 124, rue de Wantzenau.
Tel: 03-88-31-05-10.

> Carries kosher items. Closed Sunday.

Bookstores

Fraenckel. 19, rue du Maréchal Foch.
Tel: 03-88-36-38-39.

Schne-Or. 15, rue de Bitche. Tel: 03-88-37-32-37.

Lectures

The Andre Neher Room. 11, rue Sellenick, at the
University of Strasbourg.

> Lectures (in French) open to the public on topics of Jewish
> interest. There is a kosher cafeteria on the premises. Open
> during the school year.

COLMAR

Synagogue: 3, rue de la Cigogne. Tel: 03-89-41-38-29.

> Orthodox; daily morning and evening minyan; Shabbat
> holiday minyan.

Mikvah: Tel: 03-89-23-86-39.

Kosher food: The synagogue has a restaurant (Beth Din)
in the basement. Open Wednesday and Thursday only.
Call synagogue for information.

METZ

Synagogue: 39, rue du Rabbin-Elie-Bloch.
Tel: 03-87-75-04-44.

Orthodox; daily morning and evening minyan; Shabbat and holiday minyan.

Mikvah: 30, rue Kellerman. Tel: 03-87-32-38-04.

Kosher restaurant: In the synagogue. Open for lunch Monday–Friday.

Kosher grocery and butcher shop: 22, rue Mangin.
Tel: 03-87-63-33-50.

Kosher Takeout: Jacques. 28, rue St.-Pierre.
Tel: 03-87-62-25-29.

NANCY

Synagogue: 17, boulevard Joffre. Tel: 03-83-32-10-67.

Orthodox; daily morning minyan; services on Shabbat and festivals.

Mikvah: 53, rue Hoche. Tel: 03-83-30-38-92 or
03-83-41-34-48.

Kosher food: Inquire at the synagogue.

CHAPTER FIFTEEN

Champagne

CHAMPAGNE WAS ONCE HOME to several centers of Jewish scholarship—notably Troyes, Rashi's home.

The small community of Jews in medieval Champagne earned their living lending money to the local lords and to the monasteries. Though Jews lived in the towns of Bar-sur-Aube, Bray-sur-Seine, Châlons-sur-Marne, Château-Thierry, Châtillon-sur-Marne, Dampierre-sur-Aube, Epernay, Joigny, Joinville, Provins, Reims, Sens, and Troyes, they were under the control of the regional lords rather than the individual towns in which they lived.

The general expulsion from France in 1182 left Champagne Jews relatively unscathed, as Champagne did not become part of France until 1286. But the 1306 expulsion applied to them, too. Though some did come back toward the middle of that century, the Champagne region would never again see the kind of Jewish activity it had once known.

Reims

HISTORIANS ARE UNCERTAIN OF the location of Reims's medieval synagogue. It is believed to have been at 18, rue des Elus, a street whose name has changed over the centuries—from the Vicus Judaeorum to the rue de Gieu (a form of *Juif*) to the rue des Elus. The Jewish community goes back to the late eleventh century. Jews returned briefly some years after the general expulsion from France in 1306, and some Christian names from that era are annotated with the words *le Juif,* indicating that that person was probably a convert. A similar situation is found in Strasbourg (see the Strasbourg section of chapter 14).

There was no formal community again in Reims until 1870, when Jews from Alsace and Lorraine came to settle. On the eve of World War II some two hundred families lived here. They were all rounded up by the Germans on a single day in 1941 and deported.

SIGHTS

Cathedral

Notre Dame. Cours Anatole-France. There are two Synagoga statues on the walls of this cathedral—one above the left portal on the west, and the other above the portal on the south.

Synagogue

49, rue Clovis. Tel: 03-26-47-68-47. Built in 1871. There is a memorial plaque to those who were deported during World War II, but who did not return.

Memorial

War Memorial. Boulevard Général-Leclerc. An urn contains the ashes of concentration camp victims. Under the heading Civilian Victims of Nazi Repression, you will notice that most of the names are Jewish.

Troyes

*N*OTHING REMAINS OF THE medieval Jewish community here, which was very small in size but huge in its contribution to Judaism. Historians believe that the Saint Frobert quarter was where the Jews of the town lived. Rashi (1040–1105), one of the greatest commentators on the Torah who ever lived, resided and taught here. And Rashi's grandson, the noted Jewish scholar known as Rabbenu Tam (1100–71), held court here, too, and attracted students from all over Europe. (See chapter 1 for more on Rashi and his followers.)

SIGHTS

Synagogue

5, rue Brunneval. Located in a historic section of town, in an environment typical of the Champagne region, is a replica of a synagogue from Rashi's time. Begun in 1982, it was dedicated in 1987.

Cathedral

Cathédrale St.-Pierre et St.-Paul. Rue de la Cité. One of the walls of the cathedral has a gargoyle—a monstrous Jewish figure wearing a pointed hat and carrying a large purse on his belt.

CHAPTER SIXTEEN

Flanders-Picardy

THIS REGION WAS NEVER HOME to many Jews in the past and has only small communities today.

Amiens

SIGHTS

Cathedral

Cathédrale Notre-Dame. Place St.-Michel. In front of the main door is a Synagoga statue, but it isn't in the typical form of a blindfolded woman. Here you see it as a dying tree with an axe at its trunk.

Lille

THE COMMUNITY HERE DATES from the nineteenth century. Some thirteen hundred Jews lived here in 1942; the vast majority were refugees. The Germans, who maintained a branch of the Commissariat Général aux Questions Juives in Lille, deported most to the transit camp at Drancy, and from there to Auschwitz.

SIGHTS

Synagogue

5, rue Auguste-Angellier. Tel: 03-20-51-12-52. Built in 1871. Services daily and on Shabbat.

Notes

1. Thirza Vallois, *Around and About Paris*, London, Iliad Books, 1995.

2. *Encyclopedia Judaica*, 1st CD-ROM edition, s.v. More Judaico.

3. *Encyclopedia Judaica*, 1st CD-ROM edition, s.v. Marranos.

4. *Encyclopedia Judaica*, 1st CD-ROM edition, s.v. Adolphe Crémieux.

5. *Encyclopedia Judaica*, 1st CD-ROM edition, s.v. Mortara case.

6. *Encyclopedia Judaica*, 1st CD-ROM edition, s.v. France.

7. Heinz Schreckenberg: *Die Juden in der Kunst Europas*, Ein Bild-atlas, Göttingen, Vandenhoeck & Ruprecht, 1996.

8. Haim David Azulai, *Ma'gal Tob*. Quoted in *Jewish Travelers in the Middle Ages: 19 Firsthand Accounts*, edited by Elkan Nathan Adler, New York, Dover Publications, 1987.

9. Heinz Schreckenberg: *Die Juden in der Kunst Europas*, Ein Bild-atlas, Göttingen, Vandenhoeck & Ruprecht, 1996.

10. *Encyclopedia Judaica*, 1st CD-ROM edition, s.v. France.

11. Heinz Schreckenberg: *Die Juden in der Kunst Europas*, Ein Bild-atlas, Göttingen, Vandenhoeck & Ruprecht, 1996.

12. Consistoire Central de France, Annuaire 1999/2000, Paris, 1999.

Suggested Reading

Adler, Jacques. *The Jews of Paris and the Final Solution: Communal Response and Internal Conflicts, 1940–1944.* New York: Oxford University Press, 1987.

Berkovitz, Jay R. *The Shaping of Jewish Identity in Nineteenth-Century France.* Detroit: Wayne State University Press, 1989.

Bredin, Jean-Denis. *The[Dreyfus]Affair.* New York: W.W. Norton & Company, 1984.

Calmann, Marianne. *The Carrière of Carpentras.* Oxford: Littman Library of Jewish Civilization, 1984.

Finkielkraut, Alain. *The Imaginary Jew.* Lincoln: University of Nebraska Press, 1994.

Golb, Norman. *The Jews in Medieval Normandy: A Social and Intellectual History.* Cambridge: Cambridge University Press, 1998.

Green, Nancy L. *The Pletzl of Paris: Jewish Immigrant Workers in the Belle Epoque.* New York: Holmes & Meier, 1986.

Hallie, Philip P. *Lest Innocent Blood Be Shed: The Story of the Village of Le Chambon and How Goodness Happened There.* New York: Harper & Row, 1979.

Hertzberg, Arthur. *The French Enlightenment and the Jews: The Origins of Modern Anti-Semitism.* New York: Columbia University Press, 1968.

Hyman, Paula E. *The Emancipation of the Jews of Alsace: Acculturation and Tradition in the Nineteenth Century.* New Haven: Yale University Press, 1991.

———. *The Jews of Modern France.* Berkeley: University of California Press, 1998.

Lazare, Lucien. *Rescue As Resistance: How Jewish Organizations Fought the Holocaust in France.* Translated by Jeffrey M. Green. New York: Columbia University Press, 1996.

Malino, Frances. *A Jew in the French Revolution: The Life of Zalkind Hourwitz.* Oxford: Blackwell Publishers, 1996.

Marrus, Michael R., and Robert O. Paxton. *Vichy France and the Jews.* Stanford: Stanford University Press, 1981, 1995.

Ryan, Donna F. *The Holocaust and the Jews of Marseille: The Enforcement of Anti-Semitic Policies in Vichy France.* Champaign: University of Illinois Press, 1996.

Schnapper, Dominique. *Jewish Identities in France: An Analysis of Contemporary French Jewry.* Chicago: University of Chicago Press, 1984.

Vidal-Naquet, Pierre, and David Ames Curtis, eds. *The Jews: History, Memory, and the Present.* New York: Columbia University Press, 1996.

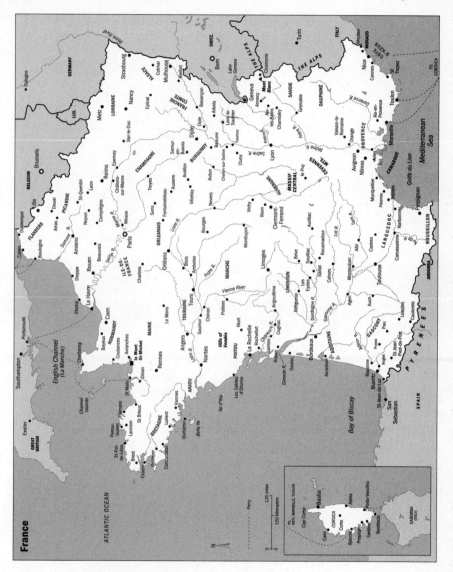

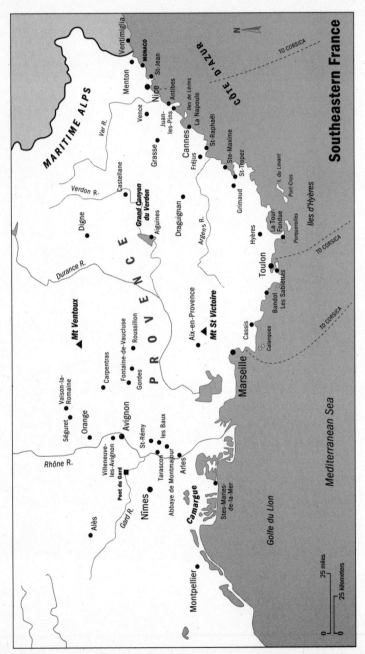

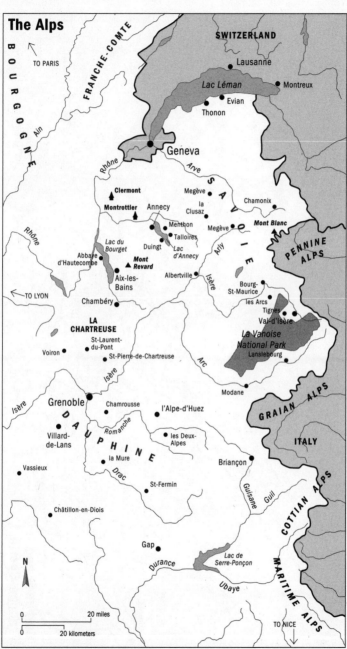

The Alps

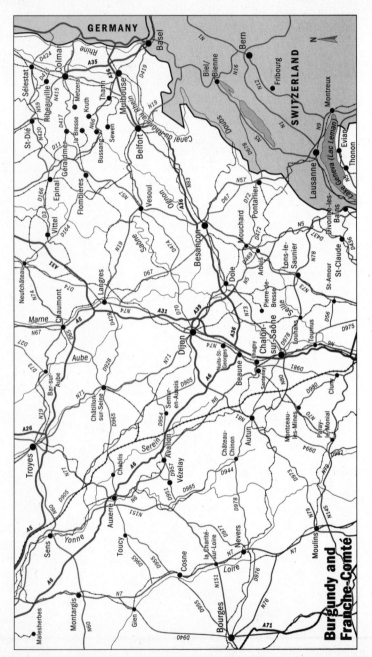

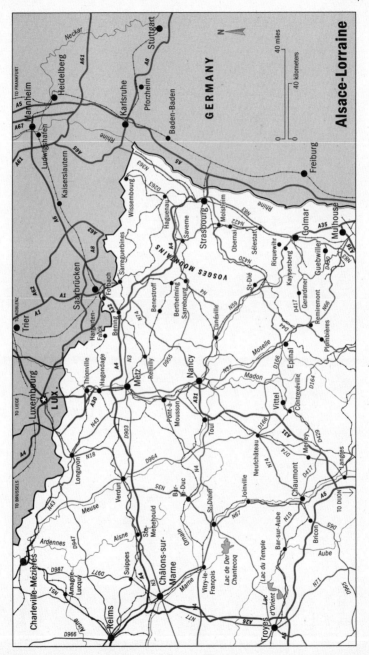

Alsace-Lorraine

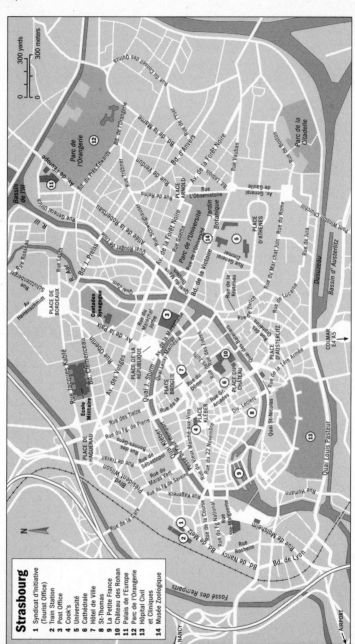

Strasbourg

1 Syndicat d'Initiative
  (Tourist Office)
2 Train Station
3 Post Office
4 Cook's
5 Université
6 Cathédrale
7 Hôtel de Ville
8 St-Thomas
9 La Petite France
10 Château des Rohan
11 Palais de l'Europe
12 Parc de l'Orangene
13 Hôpital Civil
   et Cliniques
14 Musée Zoologique

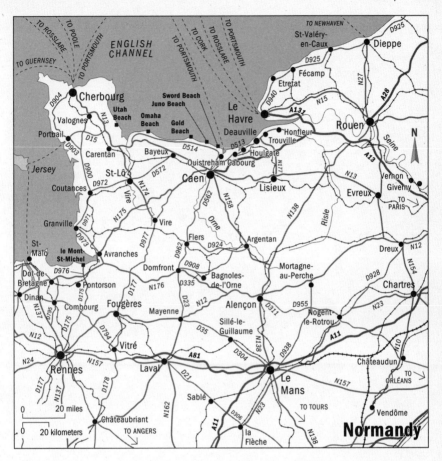

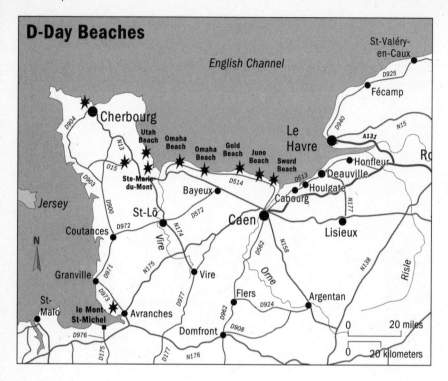

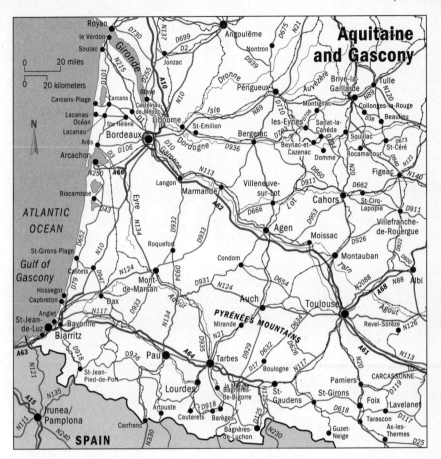

Languedoc-Roussillon

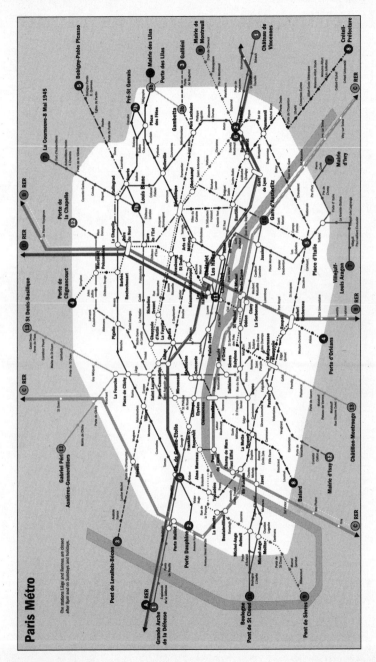

Paris Métro

The stations Liège and Rennes are closed after 8pm and on Sundays and holidays.

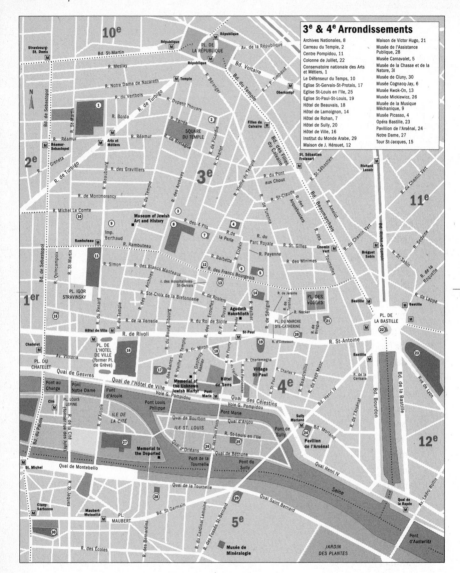

3ᵉ & 4ᵉ Arrondissements

Archives Nationales, 8
Carreau du Temple, 2
Centre Pompidou, 11
Colonne de Juillet, 22
Conservatoire nationale des Arts et Métiers, 1
Le Défenseur du Temps, 10
Eglise St-Gervais-St-Protais, 17
Eglise St-Louis en l'île, 25
Eglise St-Paul-St-Louis, 19
Hôtel de Beauvais, 18
Hôtel de Lamoignon, 14
Hôtel de Rohan, 7
Hôtel de Sully, 20
Hôtel de Ville, 16
Institut du Monde Arabe, 29
Maison de J. Hérouet, 12

Maison de Victor Hugo, 21
Musée de l'Assistance Publique, 28
Musée Carnavalet, 5
Musée de la Chasse et de la Nature, 3I
Musée de Cluny, 30
Musée Cognacq-Jay, 6
Musée Kwok-On, 13
Musée Mickiewicz, 26
Musée de la Musique Méchanique, 9
Musée Picasso, 4
Opéra Bastille, 23
Pavillion de l'Arsénal, 24
Notre Dame, 27
Tour St-Jacques, 15

Index

Page references in italics denote illustrations.

About the Author

Toni L. Kamins has Jewish travel in her genes; for hundreds of years there have been rabbis in her family, and family legend has it that she is descended from Rabbi Judah Loew of Prague, the sixteenth-century creator of the Golem. Toni teaches basic Hebrew and Judaism at her local synagogue and is an active member of the congregation. A freelance journalist and former editor, she has covered an array of Jewish and secular subjects for the *New York Times*, the *New York Daily News*, the *Jerusalem Post*, *New York* magazine, the *Village Voice*, *Forward*, and other publications as well as Web sites devoted to travel topics. Toni also edited and contributed to various major travel guides and wrote articles on the Middle East and on the Shoah for the book *Our Times: An Illustrated History of the 20th Century* (Turner Publishing).

A native New Yorker, Toni considers Paris her second home. She has degrees in history and political science from Hunter College and the City University of New York and has studied at the Institute of Political Studies in Paris.

She resides in New York City with her husband. Her e-mail address is toni@completejewishguides.com.